HOA LO PRISON, HANOI, NORTH VIETNAM. 1969.

NAVY PILOT JOHN SIDNEY McCAIN III IS IN PAIN. TWO YEARS EARLIER, BOTH HIS ARMS AND HIS RIGHT LEG WERE BROKEN WHEN HIS PLANE WAS SHOT DOWN WHILE ON A BOMBING RUN OVER HANOI.

ACCORDED THE BARE MINIMUM OF MEDICAL CARE BY HIS NORTH VIETNAMESE CAPTORS, McCAIN HAS ESSENTIALLY BEEN TOLD TO MAKE DO.

THE FACT THAT HE HAS SURVIVED AT ALL CAME AS A SURPRISE TO THE POORLY TRAINED, ILL-EQUIPPED NORTH VIETNAMESE MEDICS; THEY BELIEVED HE WAS ALREADY TOO FAR GONE TO BE SAVED.

BUT AGAINST ALL ODDS, McCAIN SURVIVED. DESPITE THE PRISON'S PITIABLE ACCOMMODATIONS, SADISTIC GUARDS, PRIMITIVE MEDICAL FACILITIES, AND SUBSISTENT RATIONS, ALL OF WHICH SEEMED TO CONSPIRE TO HINDER ANY PROSPECT FOR HIS EVENTUAL RECOVERY, JOHN McCAIN SURVIVED.

LONG ENOUGH FOR HIM TO BE ASSIGNED HIS OWN CELL. WHERE HE SITS. AND WILL CONTINUE TO SIT. FOR OVER THIRTY MONTHS. ALONE. IN PAIN.

IN SOLITARY.

FOR MONTHS FOLLOWING HIS ARRIVAL AT THE HOA LO, McCAIN'S ONLY CONTACT WITH OTHER HUMAN BEINGS WAS WITH HIS CAPTORS, WHO SUBJECTED HIM TO AN ENDLESS SERIES OF ACCUSATIONS AND INTERROGATIONS.

AT VARIOUS TIMES THEY DEMANDED THAT McCAIN REVEAL MILITARY SECRETS, CONFESS TO COMMITTING "BLACK CRIMES" AGAINST THE NORTH VIETNAMESE GOVERNMENT, AND FEED THE NORTH'S PROPAGANDA EFFORTS BY ADMITTING THE ERROR OF HIS WAYS, BEGGING FORGIVENESS, AND THANKING THE VIETNAMESE PEOPLE FOR THEIR COMPASSIONATE TREATMENT.

WHEN McCAIN REFUSED TO COOPERATE, THE TORTURE BEGAN.

HIS FRAIL ARMS AND LEGS BECAME TARGETS FOR THE GUARDS' ATTACKS. HIS ARM WAS BROKEN AGAIN.

HIS RIBS WERE CRACKED. FOR DAYS, SEVERE BEATINGS WERE ADMINISTERED EVERY FEW HOURS.

AT TIMES HE WAS FORCED TO STAND FOR HOURS ON END. AT OTHERS, HE WAS PLACED ON A STOOL AND BOUND IN ROPES THAT STRETCHED HIS DAMAGED ARMS BEHIND HIS BACK TO A PAINFUL BREAKING POINT.

"EVERY MAN HAS HIS BREAKING POINT," McCAIN HAS SAID. "I HAD REACHED MINE." HE SAW ONLY TWO CHOICES BEFORE HIM NOW: SUICIDE, OR CONFESSION.

WHILE CHOOSING THE LATTER, HE STROVE TO DILUTE THE MESSAGES HIS CAPTORS WANTED HIM TO CONVEY.

PERHAPS, HE BELIEVED, IT MIGHT SALVAGE SOME SMALL MEASURE OF HIS DIGNITY.

THE TORTURE SESSIONS RAN ALMOST CONTINUOUSLY; AT TIMES, IT MIGHT SEEM TO McCAIN THAT HE HAD LITTLE IN LIFE TO LOOK FORWARD TO BEYOND EXPERIENCING PERVERSE NEW VARIATIONS ON NIGHTMARISH TORTURE TECHNIQUES.

McCAIN'S REWARD FOR SIGNING HIS FORCED "CONFESSION" WAS A TEMPORARY REPRIEVE.

HE USED THE TIME TO RECUPERATE, GET A "SECOND WIND," AND RESOLVE TO NEVER COMPROMISE HIS DUTY TO HIS COUNTRY AGAIN.

RETURNED TO HIS CELL, McCAIN WAS CONFRONTED WITH AN EVEN HARSHER FATE: THE ISOLATION AND LONELINESS OF SOLITARY CONFINEMENT. PRISONERS SELDOM SAW EACH OTHER. AND SPEAKING WAS FORBIDDEN. BUT THEY OVERCAME THIS BY TAPPING OUT CODED MESSAGES ON WALLS AND PIPES.

THE BITS OF ENCODED CHATTER TRANSMITTED FROM CELL TO CELL, McCAIN BELIEVES, WAS THE LIFELINE THAT KEPT HIM SANE DURING HIS FIVE-YEAR ORDEAL. THAT, AND HIS MEMORIES.

"WHEN YOU'RE LEFT ALONE WITH YOUR THOUGHTS FOR YEARS," McCAIN WROTE YEARS LATER, "IT'S HARD NOT TO REFLECT ON HOW BETTER YOU COULD HAVE SPENT YOUR TIME AS A FREE MAN."

AND SO, HE DID.

THERE'S LITTLE ARGUMENT THAT JOHN McCAIN HAD A DESTINY TO FULFILL. ONE CAN DEBATE EXACTLY WHAT THAT DESTINY IS, BUT ONE PARTICULAR PATH FOR HIM TO FOLLOW HAD BEEN SET GENERATIONS BEFORE HE WAS EVEN BORN.

THE McCAIN TRADITION OF MILITARY SERVICE STRETCHES EVEN FURTHER BACK THAN HIS GREAT-GREAT GRANDFATHER WILLIAM ALEXANDER McCAIN, A CARROLL COUNTY, MISSISSIPPI PLANTATION OWNER WHO DIED IN THE CIVIL WAR FIGHTING WITH THE MISSISSIPPI CAVALRY.

THAT THE PLANTATION RELIED ON THE LABOR OF McCAIN'S 52 SLAVES WOULD SURPRISE HIS GREAT-GREAT GRANDSON WHEN PRESENTED WITH THE INFORMATION DURING HIS 2000 PRESIDENTIAL RUN.

I DIDN'T KNOW THAT.

--WAS THE BEST THE FLABBERGASTED McCAIN COULD MUSTER WHEN ASKED TO COMMENT ON THE EMBARRASSING DISCOVERY.

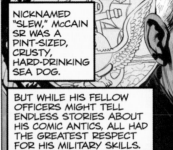

BORN IN 1884, GRANDFATHER JOHN SIDNEY McCAIN SR. ANCHORED THE FAMILY'S SERVICE TO THE NAVY. AFTER GRADUATING FROM ANNAPOLIS AT THE BOTTOM OF HIS CLASS (FORGING A TREND FOR FUTURE GENERATIONS OF McCAINS) HE ADVANCED SLOWLY BUT STEADILY TO THE RANK OF VICE-ADMIRAL.

NICKNAMED "SLEW," McCAIN SR WAS A PINT-SIZED, CRUSTY, HARD-DRINKING SEA DOG.

BUT WHILE HIS FELLOW OFFICERS MIGHT TELL ENDLESS STORIES ABOUT HIS COMIC ANTICS, ALL HAD THE GREATEST RESPECT FOR HIS MILITARY SKILLS.

1911 SAW THE ARRIVAL OF JOHN SIDNEY McCAIN JR.. LIKE FATHER "SLEW," "JUNIOR" JUST BARELY GRADUATED FROM THE U.S. NAVAL ACADEMY IN 1931. WHILE STATIONED IN THE PANAMA CANAL ZONE IN 1936, SON JOHN McCAIN III WAS BORN.

AT THE TIME, THE CANAL ZONE WAS UNITED STATES TERRITORY, SO THE YOUNGEST McCAIN WAS A U.S. CITIZEN—QUALIFIED TO RUN FOR ANY PUBLIC OFFICE.

AS YOUNG McCAIN GREW, THE TWO OLDER GENERATIONS OF McCAINS SERVED IN THE PACIFIC THEATER OF WORLD WAR II.

AS "SLEW" COMMANDED THE FAST CARRIER TASK FORCE ON THE OCEAN'S SURFACE, JUNIOR COMMANDED SUBMARINE PATROLS BELOW.

ON SEPTEMBER 2, 1945, "SLEW" McCAIN WAS ASKED TO ATTEND THE FORMAL SURRENDER OF THE JAPANESE ON THE DECK OF THE U.S.S. MISSOURI. EXHAUSTED FROM MONTHS OF COMBAT, "SLEW" TRIED TO BEG OFF, BUT HIS SUPERIORS INSISTED.

"SLEW" WAS THERE. FOUR DAYS LATER, HIS MILITARY SERVICE TO HIS COUNTRY COMPLETE, HE DIED OF A HEART ATTACK. A PROMOTION TO FULL ADMIRAL WOULD BE AWARDED POSTHUMOUSLY.

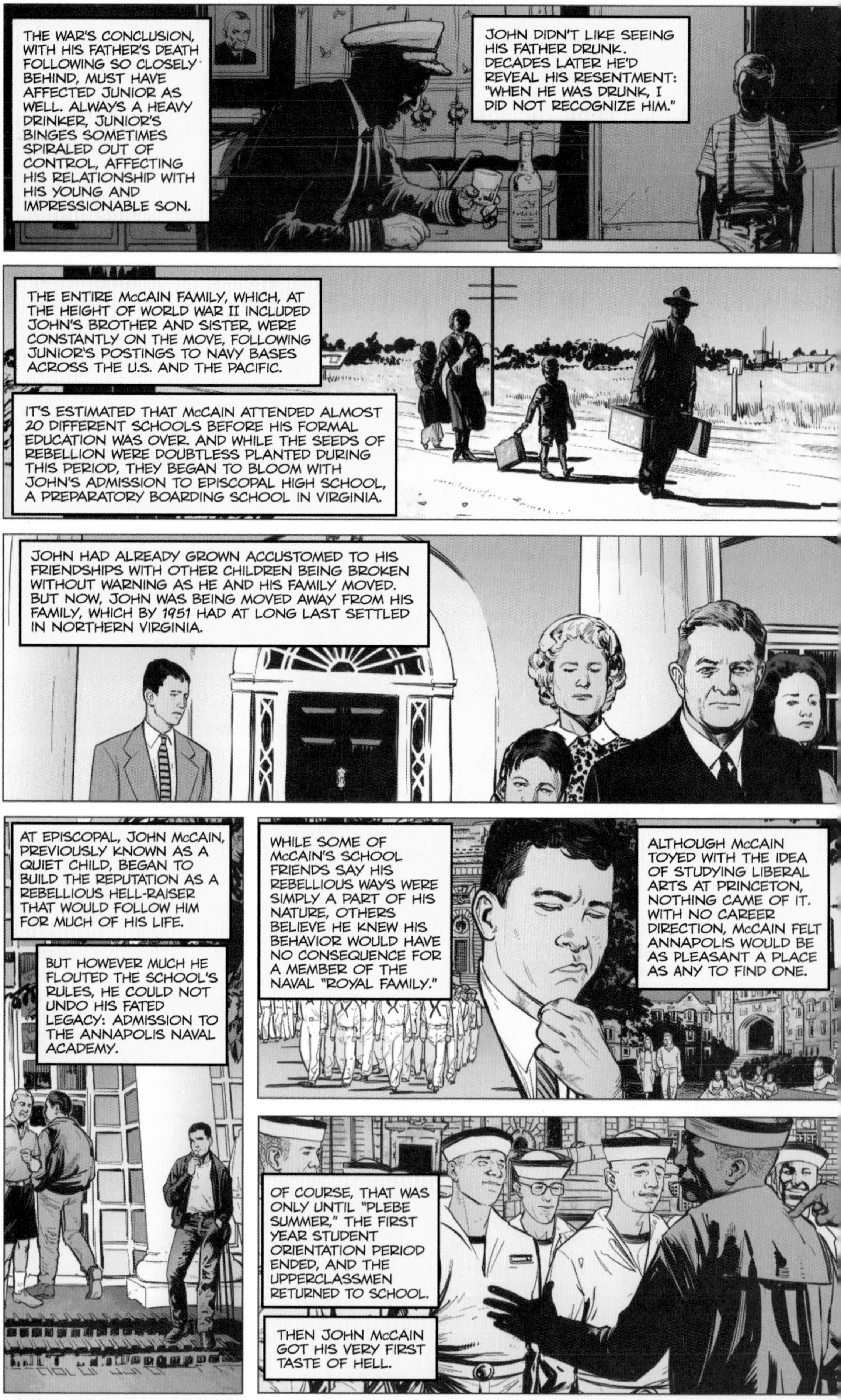
THE WAR'S CONCLUSION, WITH HIS FATHER'S DEATH FOLLOWING SO CLOSELY BEHIND, MUST HAVE AFFECTED JUNIOR AS WELL. ALWAYS A HEAVY DRINKER, JUNIOR'S BINGES SOMETIMES SPIRALED OUT OF CONTROL, AFFECTING HIS RELATIONSHIP WITH HIS YOUNG AND IMPRESSIONABLE SON.
JOHN DIDN'T LIKE SEEING HIS FATHER DRUNK. DECADES LATER HE'D REVEAL HIS RESENTMENT: "WHEN HE WAS DRUNK, I DID NOT RECOGNIZE HIM."
THE ENTIRE McCAIN FAMILY, WHICH, AT THE HEIGHT OF WORLD WAR II INCLUDED JOHN'S BROTHER AND SISTER, WERE CONSTANTLY ON THE MOVE, FOLLOWING JUNIOR'S POSTINGS TO NAVY BASES ACROSS THE U.S. AND THE PACIFIC.
IT'S ESTIMATED THAT McCAIN ATTENDED ALMOST 20 DIFFERENT SCHOOLS BEFORE HIS FORMAL EDUCATION WAS OVER. AND WHILE THE SEEDS OF REBELLION WERE DOUBTLESS PLANTED DURING THIS PERIOD, THEY BEGAN TO BLOOM WITH JOHN'S ADMISSION TO EPISCOPAL HIGH SCHOOL, A PREPARATORY BOARDING SCHOOL IN VIRGINIA.
JOHN HAD ALREADY GROWN ACCUSTOMED TO HIS FRIENDSHIPS WITH OTHER CHILDREN BEING BROKEN WITHOUT WARNING AS HE AND HIS FAMILY MOVED. BUT NOW, JOHN WAS BEING MOVED AWAY FROM HIS FAMILY, WHICH BY 1951 HAD AT LONG LAST SETTLED IN NORTHERN VIRGINIA.
AT EPISCOPAL, JOHN McCAIN, PREVIOUSLY KNOWN AS A QUIET CHILD, BEGAN TO BUILD THE REPUTATION AS A REBELLIOUS HELL-RAISER THAT WOULD FOLLOW HIM FOR MUCH OF HIS LIFE.
BUT HOWEVER MUCH HE FLOUTED THE SCHOOL'S RULES, HE COULD NOT UNDO HIS FATED LEGACY: ADMISSION TO THE ANNAPOLIS NAVAL ACADEMY.
WHILE SOME OF McCAIN'S SCHOOL FRIENDS SAY HIS REBELLIOUS WAYS WERE SIMPLY A PART OF HIS NATURE, OTHERS BELIEVE HE KNEW HIS BEHAVIOR WOULD HAVE NO CONSEQUENCE FOR A MEMBER OF THE NAVAL "ROYAL FAMILY."
ALTHOUGH McCAIN TOYED WITH THE IDEA OF STUDYING LIBERAL ARTS AT PRINCETON, NOTHING CAME OF IT. WITH NO CAREER DIRECTION, McCAIN FELT ANNAPOLIS WOULD BE AS PLEASANT A PLACE AS ANY TO FIND ONE.
OF COURSE, THAT WAS ONLY UNTIL "PLEBE SUMMER," THE FIRST YEAR STUDENT ORIENTATION PERIOD ENDED, AND THE UPPERCLASSMEN RETURNED TO SCHOOL.
THEN JOHN McCAIN GOT HIS VERY FIRST TASTE OF HELL.

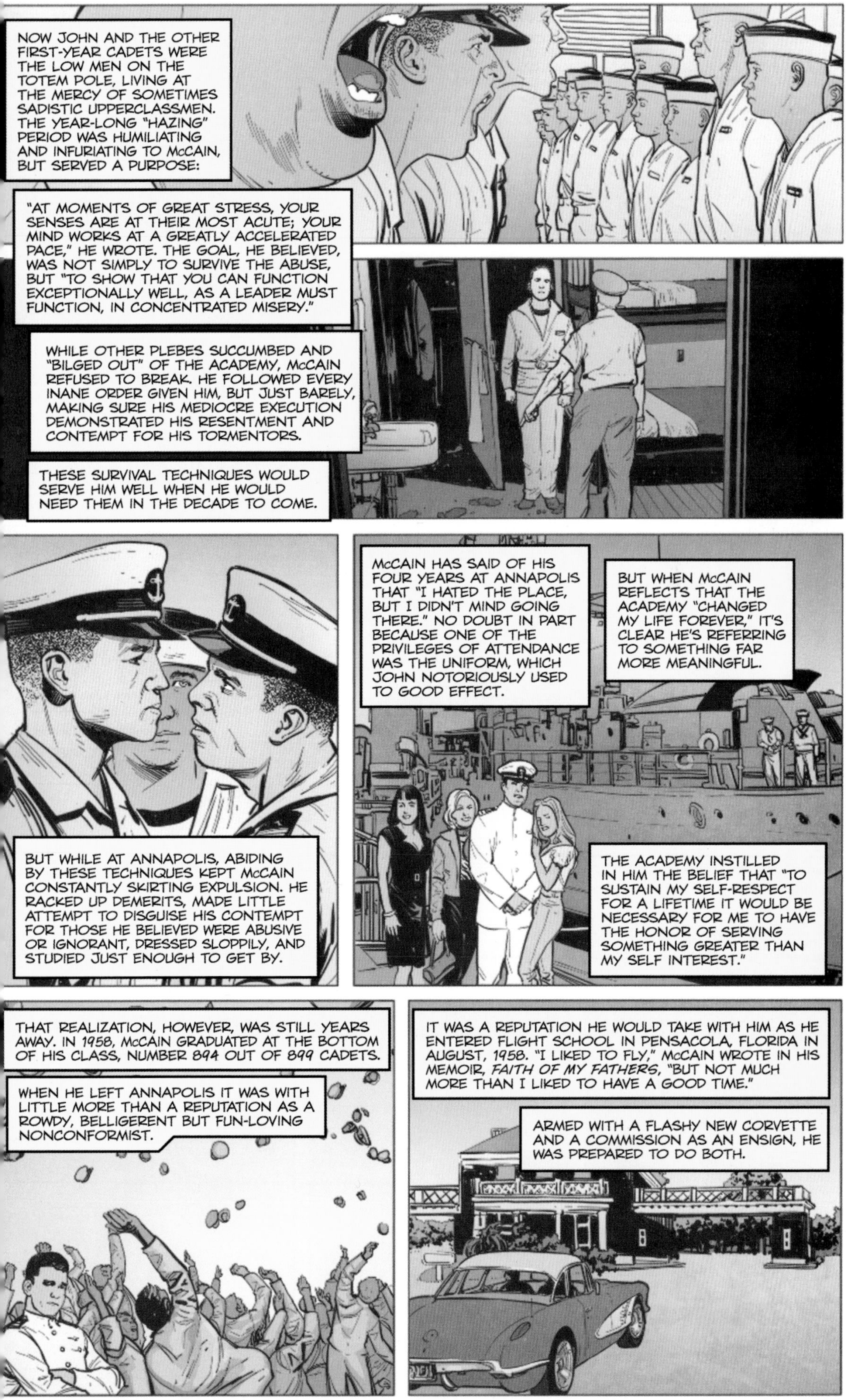
NOW JOHN AND THE OTHER FIRST-YEAR CADETS WERE THE LOW MEN ON THE TOTEM POLE, LIVING AT THE MERCY OF SOMETIMES SADISTIC UPPERCLASSMEN. THE YEAR-LONG "HAZING" PERIOD WAS HUMILIATING AND INFURIATING TO McCAIN, BUT SERVED A PURPOSE:
"AT MOMENTS OF GREAT STRESS, YOUR SENSES ARE AT THEIR MOST ACUTE; YOUR MIND WORKS AT A GREATLY ACCELERATED PACE," HE WROTE. THE GOAL, HE BELIEVED, WAS NOT SIMPLY TO SURVIVE THE ABUSE, BUT "TO SHOW THAT YOU CAN FUNCTION EXCEPTIONALLY WELL, AS A LEADER MUST FUNCTION, IN CONCENTRATED MISERY."
WHILE OTHER PLEBES SUCCUMBED AND "BILGED OUT" OF THE ACADEMY, McCAIN REFUSED TO BREAK. HE FOLLOWED EVERY INANE ORDER GIVEN HIM, BUT JUST BARELY, MAKING SURE HIS MEDIOCRE EXECUTION DEMONSTRATED HIS RESENTMENT AND CONTEMPT FOR HIS TORMENTORS.
THESE SURVIVAL TECHNIQUES WOULD SERVE HIM WELL WHEN HE WOULD NEED THEM IN THE DECADE TO COME.
BUT WHILE AT ANNAPOLIS, ABIDING BY THESE TECHNIQUES KEPT McCAIN CONSTANTLY SKIRTING EXPULSION. HE RACKED UP DEMERITS, MADE LITTLE ATTEMPT TO DISGUISE HIS CONTEMPT FOR THOSE HE BELIEVED WERE ABUSIVE OR IGNORANT, DRESSED SLOPPILY, AND STUDIED JUST ENOUGH TO GET BY.
McCAIN HAS SAID OF HIS FOUR YEARS AT ANNAPOLIS THAT "I HATED THE PLACE, BUT I DIDN'T MIND GOING THERE." NO DOUBT IN PART BECAUSE ONE OF THE PRIVILEGES OF ATTENDANCE WAS THE UNIFORM, WHICH JOHN NOTORIOUSLY USED TO GOOD EFFECT.
BUT WHEN McCAIN REFLECTS THAT THE ACADEMY "CHANGED MY LIFE FOREVER," IT'S CLEAR HE'S REFERRING TO SOMETHING FAR MORE MEANINGFUL.
THE ACADEMY INSTILLED IN HIM THE BELIEF THAT "TO SUSTAIN MY SELF-RESPECT FOR A LIFETIME IT WOULD BE NECESSARY FOR ME TO HAVE THE HONOR OF SERVING SOMETHING GREATER THAN MY SELF INTEREST."
THAT REALIZATION, HOWEVER, WAS STILL YEARS AWAY. IN 1958, McCAIN GRADUATED AT THE BOTTOM OF HIS CLASS, NUMBER 894 OUT OF 899 CADETS.
WHEN HE LEFT ANNAPOLIS IT WAS WITH LITTLE MORE THAN A REPUTATION AS A ROWDY, BELLIGERENT BUT FUN-LOVING NONCONFORMIST.
IT WAS A REPUTATION HE WOULD TAKE WITH HIM AS HE ENTERED FLIGHT SCHOOL IN PENSACOLA, FLORIDA IN AUGUST, 1958. "I LIKED TO FLY," McCAIN WROTE IN HIS MEMOIR, *FAITH OF MY FATHERS*, "BUT NOT MUCH MORE THAN I LIKED TO HAVE A GOOD TIME."
ARMED WITH A FLASHY NEW CORVETTE AND A COMMISSION AS AN ENSIGN, HE WAS PREPARED TO DO BOTH.

McCAIN LEARNED TO FLY AT PENSACOLA, BUT IN KEEPING WITH HIS STYLE, JUST BARELY. HE SEEMED MORE INTERESTED IN THE "GLAMOROUS," OFF-DUTY LIFE OF A NAVY FLIER THAN IN ACTUALLY FLYING.

TO THIS END, HIS FREE TIME WAS SPENT EITHER PARTYING ON THE BEACH OR CAVORTING WITH THE STRIPPERS AT TRADER JOHN'S, A PARTICULARLY ROWDY LOCAL BAR.

CLKK
CLKK
CLKK

BUT McCAIN WOULD PAY FOR HIS LAX ATTITUDE WHEN HE MOVED ON TO ADVANCED FLIGHT TRAINING IN CORPUS CHRISTI, TEXAS. HE WAS PRACTICING LANDINGS ONE SATURDAY WHEN HIS ENGINE SUDDENLY DIED.

MEDICAL EXAMINATIONS REVEALED McCAIN HAD SUFFERED NO SERIOUS INJURIES.

IT WAS HIS FIRST AVIATION ACCIDENT, BUT IT WOULD NOT BE HIS LAST.

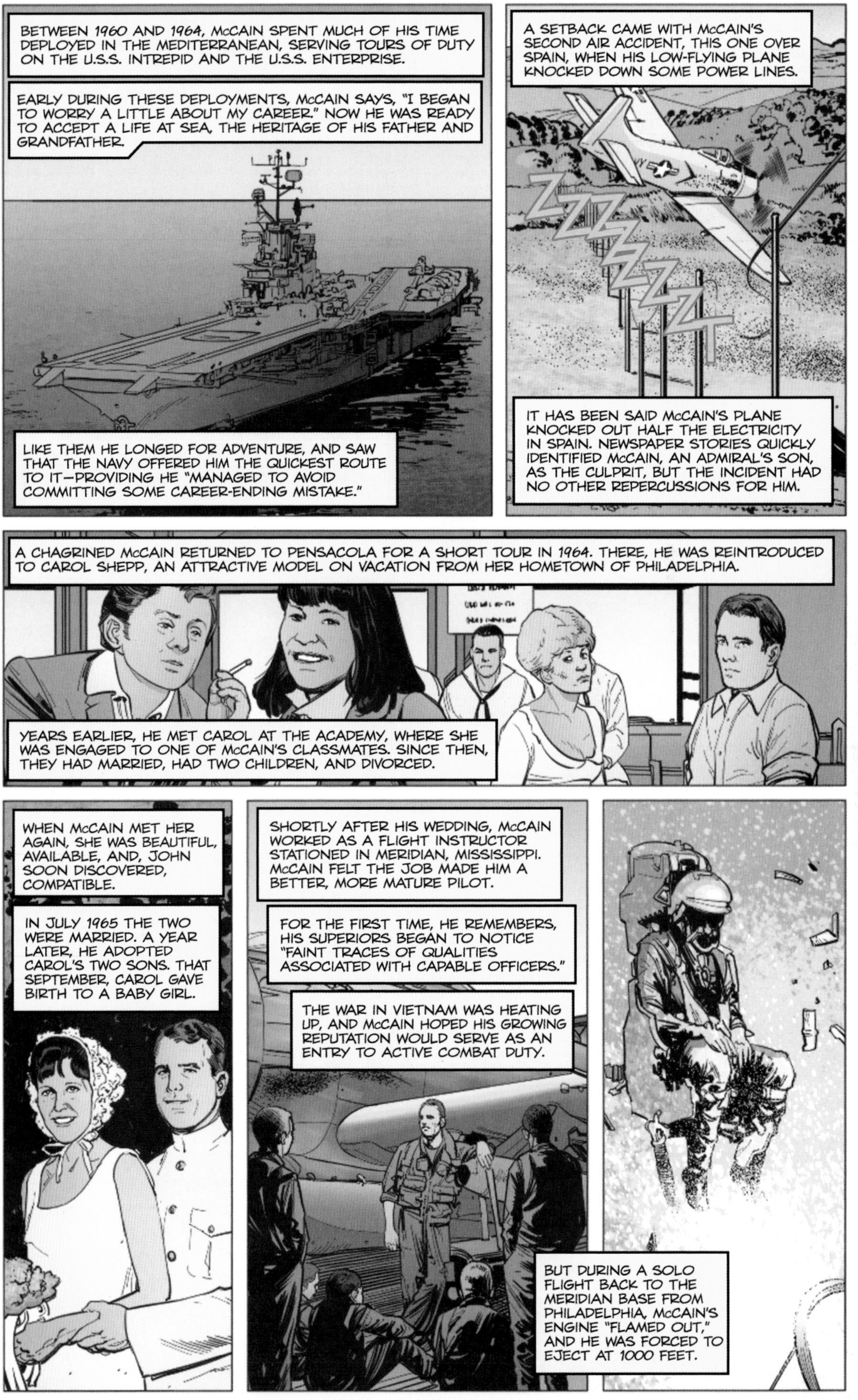
BETWEEN 1960 AND 1964, McCAIN SPENT MUCH OF HIS TIME DEPLOYED IN THE MEDITERRANEAN, SERVING TOURS OF DUTY ON THE U.S.S. INTREPID AND THE U.S.S. ENTERPRISE.
EARLY DURING THESE DEPLOYMENTS, McCAIN SAYS, "I BEGAN TO WORRY A LITTLE ABOUT MY CAREER." NOW HE WAS READY TO ACCEPT A LIFE AT SEA, THE HERITAGE OF HIS FATHER AND GRANDFATHER.
LIKE THEM HE LONGED FOR ADVENTURE, AND SAW THAT THE NAVY OFFERED HIM THE QUICKEST ROUTE TO IT—PROVIDING HE "MANAGED TO AVOID COMMITTING SOME CAREER-ENDING MISTAKE."
A SETBACK CAME WITH McCAIN'S SECOND AIR ACCIDENT, THIS ONE OVER SPAIN, WHEN HIS LOW-FLYING PLANE KNOCKED DOWN SOME POWER LINES.
IT HAS BEEN SAID McCAIN'S PLANE KNOCKED OUT HALF THE ELECTRICITY IN SPAIN. NEWSPAPER STORIES QUICKLY IDENTIFIED McCAIN, AN ADMIRAL'S SON, AS THE CULPRIT, BUT THE INCIDENT HAD NO OTHER REPERCUSSIONS FOR HIM.
A CHAGRINED McCAIN RETURNED TO PENSACOLA FOR A SHORT TOUR IN 1964. THERE, HE WAS REINTRODUCED TO CAROL SHEPP, AN ATTRACTIVE MODEL ON VACATION FROM HER HOMETOWN OF PHILADELPHIA.
YEARS EARLIER, HE MET CAROL AT THE ACADEMY, WHERE SHE WAS ENGAGED TO ONE OF McCAIN'S CLASSMATES. SINCE THEN, THEY HAD MARRIED, HAD TWO CHILDREN, AND DIVORCED.
WHEN McCAIN MET HER AGAIN, SHE WAS BEAUTIFUL, AVAILABLE, AND, JOHN SOON DISCOVERED, COMPATIBLE.
IN JULY 1965 THE TWO WERE MARRIED. A YEAR LATER, HE ADOPTED CAROL'S TWO SONS. THAT SEPTEMBER, CAROL GAVE BIRTH TO A BABY GIRL.
SHORTLY AFTER HIS WEDDING, McCAIN WORKED AS A FLIGHT INSTRUCTOR STATIONED IN MERIDIAN, MISSISSIPPI. McCAIN FELT THE JOB MADE HIM A BETTER, MORE MATURE PILOT.
FOR THE FIRST TIME, HE REMEMBERS, HIS SUPERIORS BEGAN TO NOTICE "FAINT TRACES OF QUALITIES ASSOCIATED WITH CAPABLE OFFICERS."
THE WAR IN VIETNAM WAS HEATING UP, AND McCAIN HOPED HIS GROWING REPUTATION WOULD SERVE AS AN ENTRY TO ACTIVE COMBAT DUTY.
BUT DURING A SOLO FLIGHT BACK TO THE MERIDIAN BASE FROM PHILADELPHIA, McCAIN'S ENGINE "FLAMED OUT," AND HE WAS FORCED TO EJECT AT 1000 FEET.

HE LANDED ON A DESERTED BEACH, UNINJURED.

HIS PLANE WAS DESTROYED.

THE INCIDENT GAVE McCAIN AN "UNEXPECTED GLIMPSE OF MORTALITY" WHICH MADE HIS DESIRE TO GET TO VIETNAM EVEN MORE URGENT.

HE NEEDED TO GET THERE "BEFORE SOME NEW UNFORESEEN ACCIDENT PREVENTED ME FROM EVER TAKING MY TURN IN WAR."

BY THE END OF 1966, McCAIN GOT HIS WISH. HE WAS ORDERED TO REPORT TO THE U.S.S. FORRESTAL, AND TRAIN TO FLY THE A-4 SKYHAWK, A SMALL BOMBER USED IN COMBAT MISSIONS OVER VIETNAM.

SIX MONTHS LATER, McCAIN WAS IN THE THICK OF IT. HE HAD ALREADY FLOWN FIVE SUCCESSFUL BOMBING MISSIONS FROM THE TONKIN GULF INTO VIETNAM, AND HIS MILITARY CAREER WAS AT LAST ON TRACK.

ON JULY 29, 1967, McCAIN WAS ENGAGED IN THE PREFLIGHT CHECKS FOR HIS SIXTH MISSION. TOM OTT, McCAIN'S PARACHUTE RIGGER, WIPED McCAIN'S PLASTIC HELMET VISOR CLEAN AND SHUT THE BOMBER'S CANOPY.

A STRAY ELECTRICAL CHARGE FROM A NEARBY F-14 PHANTOM IGNITED A SIX FOOT ZUNI MISSILE...

...FIRING IT DIRECTLY AT McCAIN'S AIRCRAFT.

THE MISSILE SLAMMED INTO AND IGNITED McCAIN'S 200-GALLON FUEL TANK.

WHEN McCAIN EMERGED FROM THE COCKPIT HE WAS SURROUNDED BY FLAMES. HE LEAPED OFF THE PLANE, ROLLED THROUGH A WALL OF FIRE, AND TURNED TO GET A BETTER IDEA OF WHAT HAD HAPPENED.

McCAIN REMEMBERS SEEING PETTY OFFICER GERALD FARRIER ARRIVE WITH A PORTABLE FIRE EXTINGUISHER AND TRY TO PUT OUT THE BLAZE AROUND ONE OF THE ZUNI MISSILES THAT HAD DROPPED OFF McCAIN'S PLANE.

THAT WAS WHEN THE FIRST OF THE 1000-POUND BOMBS EXPLODED.

IN THE END, 134 MEN WERE KILLED. OVER 20 PLANES WERE LOST. NINE BOMB EXPLOSIONS PENETRATED THE SHIP'S HULL. THE FUEL-FED FIRE RAGING BELOW DECKS WOULD NOT BE SUBDUED FOR 24 HOURS.

IT WOULD TAKE OVER TWO YEARS FOR THE DAMAGE DONE TO THE FORRESTAL TO BE REPAIRED. FOR THE FORRESTAL, FOR ALL INTENTS AND PURPOSES, THE WAR WAS OVER.

BUT THE WAR WAS NOT OVER FOR JOHN McCAIN. HIS GREATEST CHALLENGE WAS YET TO COME.

IN SEPTEMBER 1967, 31-YEAR-OLD LIEUTENANT COMMANDER JOHN McCAIN VOLUNTEERED TO JOIN A SHORT-HANDED FIGHTER SQUADRON ABOARD THE U.S.S. ORISKANY.

PRESIDENT JOHNSON HAD DECIDED TO ESCALATE THE WAR EFFORT, PUTTING McCAIN AND HIS BOMBERS ON THE FRONT LINE. IN A SINGLE MONTH, THEY CONDUCTED 22 BOMBING RUNS OVER NORTH VIETNAM.

ON OCTOBER 26, McCAIN'S MISSION WAS TO DESTROY A THERMAL POWER PLANT NEAR THE CENTER OF THE NORTH VIETNAMESE CAPITAL OF HANOI—SAID TO BE ONE OF THE MOST HEAVILY DEFENDED CITIES IN THE WORLD.

AS THE SQUADRON APPROACHED THE TARGET, SQUEALING RADAR-DETECTING SPEAKERS INDICATED THEY WERE BEING TRACKED BY RUSSIAN-MADE SAM MISSILES.

MREEEP
MREEEP
MREEEP

THICK CLOUDS OF ANTI-AIRCRAFT FLAK FILLED THE SKY, MAKING IT VIRTUALLY IMPOSSIBLE TO SEE THE TARGET.

OVER THE TARGET, A TONE BLARED ON THE SPEAKER, INDICATING A SAM HAD BEEN FIRED AT THE A-4. McCAIN DROPPED HIS PAYLOAD AND BEGAN A STEEP CLIMB— JUST AS A MISSILE BLEW OFF THE PLANE'S RIGHT WING.

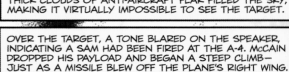

AS THE PLANE BEGAN SPIRALING DOWN TO EARTH, McCAIN RADIOED A DISTRESS MESSAGE—

I'M HIT!

—JUST BEFORE PULLING THE EJECTION SEAT HANDLE

AS HE EJECTED, HE SMASHED INTO PART OF THE PLANE—

—BREAKING HIS RIGHT ARM IN THREE PLACES, HIS LEFT ARM, AND A KNEE.

THE FORCE OF THE EJECTION PLUS, NO DOUBT, THE TREMENDOUS, UNANTICIPATED PAIN, CAUSED McCAIN TO LOSE CONSCIOUSNESS.

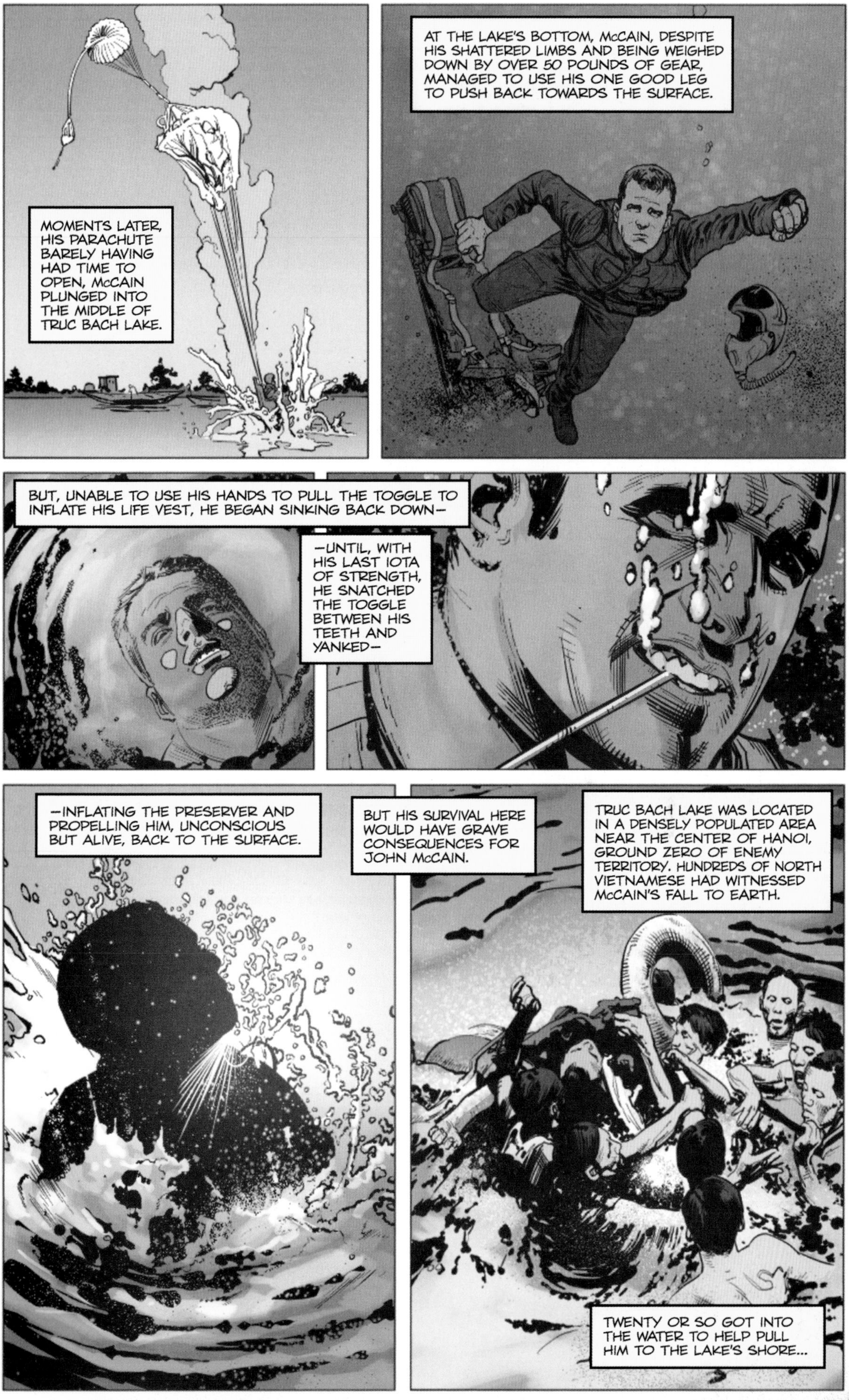
MOMENTS LATER, HIS PARACHUTE BARELY HAVING HAD TIME TO OPEN, McCAIN PLUNGED INTO THE MIDDLE OF TRUC BACH LAKE.
AT THE LAKE'S BOTTOM, McCAIN, DESPITE HIS SHATTERED LIMBS AND BEING WEIGHED DOWN BY OVER 50 POUNDS OF GEAR, MANAGED TO USE HIS ONE GOOD LEG TO PUSH BACK TOWARDS THE SURFACE.
BUT, UNABLE TO USE HIS HANDS TO PULL THE TOGGLE TO INFLATE HIS LIFE VEST, HE BEGAN SINKING BACK DOWN—
—UNTIL, WITH HIS LAST IOTA OF STRENGTH, HE SNATCHED THE TOGGLE BETWEEN HIS TEETH AND YANKED—
—INFLATING THE PRESERVER AND PROPELLING HIM, UNCONSCIOUS BUT ALIVE, BACK TO THE SURFACE.
BUT HIS SURVIVAL HERE WOULD HAVE GRAVE CONSEQUENCES FOR JOHN McCAIN.
TRUC BACH LAKE WAS LOCATED IN A DENSELY POPULATED AREA NEAR THE CENTER OF HANOI, GROUND ZERO OF ENEMY TERRITORY. HUNDREDS OF NORTH VIETNAMESE HAD WITNESSED McCAIN'S FALL TO EARTH.
TWENTY OR SO GOT INTO THE WATER TO HELP PULL HIM TO THE LAKE'S SHORE...

...AND MANY MORE WERE WAITING FOR HIM WHEN HE GOT THERE.

DAZED AND ONLY NOW BEGINNING TO FEEL THE INTENSE PAIN OF HIS BROKEN LIMBS, McCAIN COULD HARDLY HAVE BEEN EXPECTED TO ANTICIPATE WHAT WOULD COME NEXT...

...AS THE ANGRY PEASANTS UNLEASHED THEIR FURY AT HIM. "THEY BEGAN SHOUTING WILDLY AT ME," McCAIN RECALLED, "STRIPPING MY CLOTHES OFF, SPITTING ON ME, KICKING AND STRIKING ME REPEATEDLY."

DURING THE MELEE McCAIN'S SHOULDER WAS BROKEN BY A RIFLE BUTT AND HIS ANKLE WAS STABBED BY A BAYONET. BUT McCAIN REMEMBERS THAT NOT ALL THE VIETNAMESE HAD COME TO MEET HIM WITH THE SAME MURDEROUS INTENT...

...AS A WOMAN HE REMEMBERS AS A NURSE CALMED THE CROWD, GIVING HIM SOME TEA AND APPLYING CRUDE BAMBOO SPLINTS TO HIS LEG AND ARM.

HER ACTIONS DISTRACTED THE ANGRY MOB LONG ENOUGH FOR THE MILITARY TO ARRIVE AND TAKE CUSTODY OF THE FALLEN FLIER.

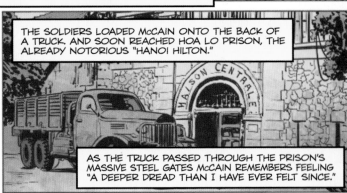

THE SOLDIERS LOADED McCAIN ONTO THE BACK OF A TRUCK. AND SOON REACHED HOA LO PRISON, THE ALREADY NOTORIOUS "HANOI HILTON."

AS THE TRUCK PASSED THROUGH THE PRISON'S MASSIVE STEEL GATES McCAIN REMEMBERS FEELING "A DEEPER DREAD THAN I HAVE EVER FELT SINCE."

ONCE INSIDE, McCAIN WAS PLACED INTO A CELL. GIVEN NOMINAL MEDICAL ATTENTION, HE DRIFTED IN AND OUT OF CONSCIOUSNESS AND WAS PERIODICALLY INTERROGATED.

IF McCAIN COOPERATED, HIS CAPTORS PROMISED HE WOULD BE HOSPITALIZED. BUT HE REFUSED, OFFERING ONLY HIS NAME, RANK AND SERIAL NUMBER.

FOR FOUR DAYS McCAIN HOVERED BETWEEN LIFE AND DEATH, HIS PLEAS FOR HELP IGNORED. BUT THEN, HIS INTERROGATION TOOK AN UNEXPECTED TURN:

YOUR FATHER IS A BIG ADMIRAL?

YES, MY FATHER IS AN ADMIRAL.

NOW WE TAKE YOU TO THE HOSPITAL.

McCAIN'S "NAME, RANK AND SERIAL NUMBER" ALONE HAD BEEN ENOUGH TO REVEAL HIM TO THE NORTH VIETNAMESE AS A VALUABLE "BARGAINING CHIP" WORTH KEEPING ALIVE.

THE VIETNAMESE BELIEVED FREEING THE ADMIRAL'S SON WOULD BE GOOD PROPAGANDA, BUT McCAIN TURNED DOWN THEIR OFFERS, DEFIANTLY CITING THE "FIRST IN, FIRST OUT" RULE, WHICH SAID P.O.W.s MUST BE RELEASED IN THE ORDER THEY'D BEEN CAPTURED.

SO McCAIN REMAINED IMPRISONED, ISOLATED FROM BOTH HIS FELLOW P.O.W.s AND THE REST OF THE WORLD...

AS THE YEARS PASSED, THE U.S. ENDURED GREAT CULTURAL AND SOCIAL UPHEAVALS, MANY INCITED BY EVENTS IN VIETNAM. ON MARCH 16, 1968, OVER 350 UNARMED CIVILIANS WERE MURDERED BY AMERICAN SOLDIERS IN THE SOUTH VIETNAMESE VILLAGE OF MY LAI.

TWO WEEKS LATER, PRESIDENT LYNDON JOHNSON, REALIZING HIS PLAN TO WIN THE WAR HAD FAILED, ANNOUNCED HE WOULD NOT SEEK REELECTION.

THE SUBSEQUENT ASSASSINATIONS OF MARTIN LUTHER KING AND PRESIDENTIAL CANDIDATE ROBERT KENNEDY FURTHER THREW THE COUNTRY INTO TURMOIL.

BY AUGUST, THE CHICAGO DEMOCRATIC CONVENTION WAS MARKED BY BLOODY RIOTS BETWEEN POLICE AND DEMONSTRATORS.

THAT FALL, REPUBLICAN RICHARD NIXON WAS ELECTED PRESIDENT, AND SOON EXTENDED THE VIETNAM WAR FRONT INTO NEIGHBORING LAOS AND CAMBODIA, COUNTRIES HE BELIEVED TO BE HARBORING NORTH VIETNAMESE FORCES.

ON MAY 4, 1970, FOUR STUDENTS AT KENT STATE UNIVERSITY IN OHIO WERE KILLED BY NATIONAL GUARD TROOPS CALLED IN TO STOP STUDENT UNREST. THE SHOOTINGS LED TO A NATIONWIDE STUDENT STRIKE OBSERVED BY OVER 4 MILLION PROTESTORS.

AND THROUGH IT ALL, THE WAR'S CASUALTIES MOUNTED. PEACE TALKS WITH THE NORTH, BEGUN BY JOHNSON, WERE CONTINUED BY NIXON AND HIS LEAD NEGOTIATOR, HENRY KISSINGER.

ON JANUARY 23, 1973, NIXON ANNOUNCED "PEACE WITH HONOR" HAD BEEN REACHED: WITHIN 60 DAYS, ALL U.S. TROOPS WOULD BE WITHDRAWN, AND ALL P.O.W.s RELEASED. SOUTH VIETNAM, THE PLAN PROMISED, WOULD REMAIN INDEPENDENT.

TWO YEARS LATER, HOWEVER, THE NORTH WOULD INVADE THE SOUTH TO UNIFY VIETNAM AS A SINGLE, COMMUNIST COUNTRY.

BUT TWO YEARS BEFORE THAT, ON MARCH 14, 1973, JOHN McCAIN WAS WELCOMED HOME.

WHILE HIS CAPTORS KEPT McCAIN UNAWARE OF ALL BUT HEAVILY BIASED ACCOUNTS OF NATIONAL NEWS, THE MOST TRAGIC STORY HAD BEEN KEPT SECRET FROM HIM BY ITS CASUALTY—HIS WIFE CAROL.

ON CHRISTMAS EVE, 1969, SHE HAD BEEN IN AN AUTOMOBILE ACCIDENT; HER INJURIES LEFT HER LARGELY DISABLED. BUT WHEN ASKED IF SHE WANTED HER HUSBAND TO BE NOTIFIED OF HER CONDITION, SHE REFUSED; SHE DIDN'T WANT TO ADD TO HIS BURDENS.

A P.O.W. RELEASED BEFORE McCAIN HAD ALREADY TOLD HIM OF HIS WIFE'S CONDITION, WHICH PREPARED HIM TO SEE THE FORMER MODEL LOOKING NOT MUCH HEALTHIER THAN McCAIN HIMSELF.

BUT McCAIN TOOK A PROACTIVE APPROACH; AFTER A SHORT HOLIDAY TO REKINDLE THEIR RELATIONSHIP, THEY BEGAN A COURSE OF PHYSICAL THERAPY.

MUCH OF McCAIN'S EFFORTS WERE DIRECTED TOWARDS RESUMING HIS NAVAL CAREER. ABOVE ALL ELSE, HE WANTED TO FLY AGAIN.

McCAIN KNEW THE NAVY MADE ALLOWANCES FOR FORMER P.O.W.s WHO WANTED TO BE PLACED IN CERTAIN MILITARY POSITIONS. TO THIS END, HE USED HIS CLOUT AS PERHAPS THE MOST FAMOUS OF ALL P.O.W.s (AND THE SON OF AN ADMIRAL) TO GAIN ADMITTANCE TO THE NATIONAL WAR COLLEGE.

THROUGH HIS READINGS THERE HE CAME TO UNDERSTAND THE HISTORY AND CAUSES OF THE VIETNAM CONFLICT, WHICH HELPED HIM COME TO TERMS WITH HIS ORDEAL.

Hell In A Very
street without j
THE BEST AND THE BE

IN 1974 HE ACCEPTED AN INVITATION TO VISIT SAIGON TO ADDRESS THE SOUTH VIETNAMESE WAR COLLEGE.

DESPITE THE STUDENTS' OPTIMISM, McCAIN BELIEVED THAT SOONER OR LATER THE NORTH WOULD INVADE THE SOUTH. BUT HE COULD SAY NOTHING. AMERICA MIGHT HAVE ABANDONED SOUTH VIETNAM, BUT HE WAS STILL AN AMERICAN.

ON HIS RETURN HOME, McCAIN WAS GIVEN HIS DREAM ASSIGNMENT: EXECUTIVE OFFICER OF REPLACEMENT AIR GROUP 174.

HERE HE WOULD TRAIN PILOTS DESTINED TO BE ASSIGNED TO AIRCRAFT CARRIERS, AND AS A TRAINER HE EXCELLED—

—SO MUCH SO THAT BY THE END OF HIS TOUR HIS GROUP RECEIVED A MERITORIOUS UNIT CITATION.

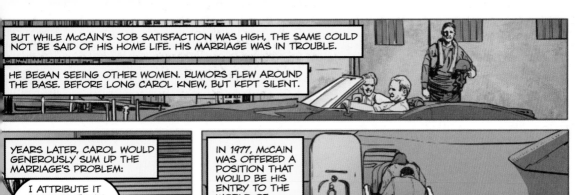

BUT WHILE McCAIN'S JOB SATISFACTION WAS HIGH, THE SAME COULD NOT BE SAID OF HIS HOME LIFE. HIS MARRIAGE WAS IN TROUBLE.

HE BEGAN SEEING OTHER WOMEN. RUMORS FLEW AROUND THE BASE. BEFORE LONG CAROL KNEW, BUT KEPT SILENT.

YEARS LATER, CAROL WOULD GENEROUSLY SUM UP THE MARRIAGE'S PROBLEM:

I ATTRIBUTE IT MORE TO JOHN TURNING 40 AND WANTING TO BE 25 AGAIN THAN I DO TO ANYTHING ELSE.

BUT THIS "MID-LIFE CRISIS" WOULD LEAD TO PERMANENT CHANGES FOR THE McCAIN FAMILY.

IN 1977, McCAIN WAS OFFERED A POSITION THAT WOULD BE HIS ENTRY TO THE WORLD OF POLITICS: NAVY LIAISON TO THE U.S. SENATE.

THE LIAISON OFFICE PERFORMED A VARIETY OF FUNCTIONS, FROM LOBBYING SENATORS TO INCREASE FUNDING FOR NAVY PROGRAMS, TO OVERSEEING INTERNATIONAL BUSINESS TRIPS BY SENATORS (AND VERY OFTEN, THEIR WIVES.)

MOST IMPORTANT, McCAIN HAD THE OPPORTUNITY TO MEET MANY OF THE MOST POWERFUL POLITICIANS IN THE NATION. HE LATER COUNTED SENATE STALWARTS BARRY GOLDWATER, JOHN STENNIS, HENRY "SCOOP" JACKSON, JOHN TOWER, AND SAM NUNN AMONG THE "PATRIOTS OF THE FIRST ORDER" HE CAME TO LEARN FROM AND ADMIRE.

AND THE ADMIRATION WAS MUTUAL. INTELLIGENCE AND EXPERIENCE ASIDE, McCAIN WAS KNOWN AS A FUN GUY TO BE AROUND, ESPECIALLY BY SENATORS WHO WERE MEMBERS OF THE VARIOUS MILITARY APPROPRIATIONS COMMITTEES HE'D LOBBY.

McCAIN WAS AN EFFECTIVE NAVY LOBBYIST. HE WAS SO POPULAR WITH THE SENATORS THAT IT WAS OFTEN REQUESTED THAT HE ACCOMPANY THEM ON THEIR INTERNATIONAL TRIPS.

OF COURSE, THESE TRIPS WERE USUALLY NOT ALL BUSINESS.

IT WAS DURING ONE OF THESE TRIPS THAT McCAIN MET CINDY HENSLEY.

McCAIN WAS INSTANTLY SMITTEN BY CINDY, 18 YEARS HIS JUNIOR. LATER, HE FOUND OUT SHE WAS THE ONLY DAUGHTER OF JIM HENSLEY, THE WEALTHY ARIZONA BEER DISTRIBUTOR.

IN APRIL 1979, WHEN McCAIN MET CINDY, HIS TRIAL SEPARATION WITH WIFE CAROL HAD FAILED TO REUNITE THEM.

AND HIS LINGERING DISABILITIES DISQUALIFIED HIM FROM BECOMING AN ADMIRAL LIKE PRECEDING GENERATIONS OF HIS FAMILY.

BOTH HIS MARRIAGE AND HIS CAREER HAD RUN AGROUND—AND WHETHER CONSCIOUS OF IT OR NOT, CINDY HENSLEY WOULD ULTIMATELY PROVIDE McCAIN WITH BOTH THE OPPORTUNITY AND THE MEANS TO REINVENT HIMSELF FOR A FUTURE IN ELECTORAL POLITICS.

IN APRIL 1980, McCAIN AND WIFE CAROL WERE DIVORCED. A MONTH LATER, HE AND CINDY WERE MARRIED.

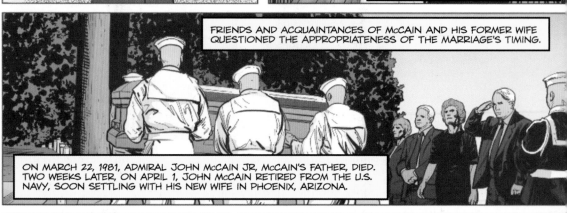

FRIENDS AND ACQUAINTANCES OF McCAIN AND HIS FORMER WIFE QUESTIONED THE APPROPRIATENESS OF THE MARRIAGE'S TIMING.

ON MARCH 22, 1981, ADMIRAL JOHN McCAIN JR, McCAIN'S FATHER, DIED. TWO WEEKS LATER, ON APRIL 1, JOHN McCAIN RETIRED FROM THE U.S. NAVY, SOON SETTLING WITH HIS NEW WIFE IN PHOENIX, ARIZONA.

JAMES W. HENSLEY, McCAIN'S FATHER-IN-LAW, GREETED HIS NEWEST FAMILY MEMBER WITH A TAILOR-MADE JOB. McCAIN WAS MADE VICE PRESIDENT OF PUBLIC RELATIONS FOR HENSLEY & COMPANY, THE FAMILY'S ANHEUSER-BUSCH DISTRIBUTORSHIP.

THE JOB ALLOWED McCAIN TO MINGLE WITH "THE PHOENIX 40," AN INFLUENTIAL GROUP OF BANKERS, LAWYERS, AND BUSINESSMEN WHOSE SUPPORT WOULD BE CRUCIAL TO HIS POLITICAL ASPIRATIONS.

AMONG THE POWER BROKERS TO REACH OUT TO SUPPORT McCAIN WAS DARROW "DUKE" TULLY, PUBLISHER OF *THE ARIZONA REPUBLIC*, THE STATE'S MOST INFLUENTIAL NEWSPAPER, AND SAVINGS & LOAN OPERATOR CHARLES H. KEATING.

ASIDE FROM NETWORKING, McCAIN LAID FURTHER POLITICAL GROUNDWORK BY CRISS-CROSSING THE PHOENIX AREA DELIVERING SPEECHES ON PATRIOTISM AND THE VALUE OF PUBLIC SERVICE.

IN 1982, POPULATION GROWTH IN ARIZONA WAS ABOUT TO NECESSITATE A NEW CONGRESSIONAL DISTRICT. HOPING THE LINES WOULD BE DRAWN NEAR HIS HOME BASE OF PHOENIX, McCAIN WAS DISAPPOINTED TO FIND THE NEW DISTRICT WOULD BE ESTABLISHED IN THE SOUTH PART OF THE STATE.

BUT WHEN A HOUSE SEAT WAS VACATED IN THE FIRST DISTRICT JUST OUTSIDE THE McCAIN HOME IN PHOENIX, CINDY QUICKLY PURCHASED A NEW HOME THERE SO JOHN WOULD QUALIFY FOR THE RACE. "I WAS GOING TO RUN," McCAIN LATER WROTE, "AND NO ONE AND NOTHING WAS GOING TO PERSUADE ME OTHERWISE."

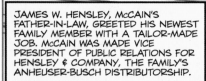

1st District

THIS FIERCE, UNRELENTING DETERMINATION TO RUN FOR OFFICE REGARDLESS OF THE CIRCUMSTANCES, LED TO CHARGES OF "CARPET-BAGGING" WHICH HOUNDED McCAIN DURING THE REPUBLICAN PRIMARY UNTIL HE DEFLATED THE ISSUE BY RESPONDING:

I WISH I COULD HAVE HAD THE LUXURY, LIKE YOU, OF GROWING UP AND LIVING AND SPENDING MY ENTIRE LIFE IN A NICE PLACE LIKE THE FIRST DISTRICT OF ARIZONA, BUT I WAS DOING OTHER THINGS.

AS A MATTER OF FACT, WHEN I THINK ABOUT IT NOW, THE PLACE I LIVED LONGEST IN MY LIFE WAS HANOI.

McCAIN LIKES TO THINK THIS OUTBURST DURING THE CANDIDATE'S DEBATE WAS THE REASON HE CARRIED THE PRIMARY OVER HIS REPUBLICAN RIVALS, BUT CLEARLY, CAMPAIGN FINANCE ALSO PLAYED A PART.

THE ARIZONA REPUBLIC
Our Candidate:
John McCain

MONEY RAISED FOR THE CAMPAIGN BY CHARLES KEATING, AS WELL AS A $167,000 LOAN FROM HIS WIFE HELPED, AS DID THE ENDORSEMENT OF TULLY'S INFLUENTIAL NEWSPAPER.

AS THE REPUBLICAN PRIMARY APPROACHED, ONE OF THE CANDIDATES, STATE SENATOR JIM MACK, CONTACTED CAROL McCAIN, WONDERING IF SHE'D HAD ANY "NEGATIVE INFORMATION" ABOUT HER EX-HUSBAND SHE MIGHT WANT TO SHARE. CAROL WAS APPALLED—AND WHEN McCAIN FOUND OUT, HE CONFRONTED MACK:

YOU EVER DO ANYTHING LIKE THAT AGAIN, ANYTHING AGAINST A PERSON IN MY FAMILY, I WILL PERSONALLY BEAT THE $%@# OUT OF YOU.

McCAIN CARRIED THE FOUR-WAY RACE, WITH 32 PERCENT OF THE VOTE, AND FOLLOWED IT IN THE GENERAL ELECTION WITH AN EASY VICTORY OVER HIS DEMOCRATIC OPPONENT. IN JANUARY 1983 THE NEWLY ELECTED FRESHMAN CONGRESSMAN FROM ARIZONA WOULD ARRIVE IN WASHINGTON D.C., THERE TO BEGIN HIS POLITICAL CAREER IN EARNEST.

McCAIN KNEW PRESIDENT RONALD REAGAN FROM YEARS BEFORE, WHEN REAGAN WAS STILL CALIFORNIA GOVERNOR AND McCAIN A RECENTLY RELEASED P.O.W. THE TWO WERE ALREADY GOOD FRIENDS.

THEIR RELATIONSHIP HAD COOLED WHEN THE McCAINS DIVORCED, AS NANCY REAGAN HAD HIRED CAROL TO WORK AT THE WHITE HOUSE SHORTLY AFTER THE TWO COUPLES FIRST MET. BUT PROFESSIONALLY AT LEAST, THE PRESIDENT AND McCAIN STILL SAW EYE TO EYE ON ALL MAJOR ISSUES EXCEPT ONE:

THE AMERICAN MILITARY'S INVOLVEMENT IN LEBANON.

MARINES WERE THERE TO SUBDUE WARRING SYRIAN AND ISRAELI FORCES. WHEN REAGAN ASKED CONGRESS TO STATION 1600 MARINES IN LEBANON, McCAIN REFUSED TO SUPPORT THE RESOLUTION, BELIEVING THE TROOP LEVEL TO BE DANGEROUSLY SMALL.

BUT THE RESOLUTION PASSED. A MONTH LATER, SUICIDE BOMBERS BLEW UP THE MARINE BARRACKS IN BEIRUT, KILLING 241 MARINES. FOR JOHN McCAIN, IT WAS A BITTER VINDICATION.

BUT McCAIN'S DECISION TO VOTE HIS CONSCIENCE RATHER THAN ALONG PARTY LINES HAD UNEXPECTED CAREER BENEFITS AS THE MEDIA SUDDENLY BEGAN PAYING ATTENTION TO THE FRESHMAN CONGRESSMAN.

SOURCES AS DIVERSE AS *U.S. NEWS & WORLD REPORT* AND *ROLLING STONE* ALL PRAISED McCAIN'S OBJECTIVITY AND INDEPENDENCE AND THANKS TO HIS ALMOST PROPHETIC STANCE HE WAS SOON BEING CONSIDERED AN EXPERT ON FOREIGN AFFAIRS.

AFTER BEING EASILY REELECTED TO THE HOUSE IN 1984, McCAIN DECIDED IN 1985 TO RETURN TO VIETNAM, THE SOURCE OF HIS GREATEST PAIN AND SACRIFICE.

ACCOMPANIED BY FAMED TV ANCHORMAN WALTER CRONKITE, McCAIN'S TOUR OF HANOI AND THE HANOI HILTON WAS FILMED FOR A DOCUMENTARY ABOUT THE LEGACY OF VIETNAM, AND McCAIN'S PRESENCE IN IT ONLY HELPED CEMENT HIS REPUTATION AS A HEROIC SURVIVOR.

WITH THESE CREDENTIALS, McCAIN SET HIS SIGHTS ON HIS NEXT OBJECTIVE: THE SENATE.

ARIZONA SENATOR BARRY GOLDWATER, 1964'S REPUBLICAN PRESIDENTIAL CHALLENGER AGAINST LYNDON JOHNSON, AND LONG KNOWN AS THE LEADER OF THE CONSERVATIVE MOVEMENT IN AMERICA, HAD ANNOUNCED HE WOULD NOT RUN FOR THE SENATE IN 1986.

McCAIN'S BIGGEST POTENTIAL RIVAL, DEMOCRATIC GOVERNOR BRUCE BABBITT, SAW HIS POSSIBLE ELECTION TO THE SENATE AS THE NEXT STEP ON HIS OWN LONGER JOURNEY TO THE WHITE HOUSE.

BUT HE ALSO KNEW THAT IF HE LOST TO McCAIN, HIS ULTIMATE GOAL MIGHT BE FOREVER BEYOND HIS GRASP—AND WITH "DUKE" TULLY AND HIS INFLUENTIAL NEWSPAPERS IN McCAIN'S CORNER, THAT COULD BE A DISTINCT POSSIBILITY. SO GOVERNOR BABBITT PASSED.

SOON, THE ONLY CANDIDATE LEFT IN McCAIN'S PATH WAS DEMOCRATIC CANDIDATE RICHARD KIMBALL. FROM THE OUTSET, HIS CHANCES AGAINST McCAIN WERE SLIM AT BEST.

THEY ONLY WORSENED WHEN THE TULLY PRESS MACHINE ROLLED OUT, NOT ONLY TO SUPPORT McCAIN, BUT TO BERATE KIMBALL FOR, AMONG OTHER THINGS, DISPLAYING "TERMINAL WEIRDNESS." KIMBALL NEEDED TO RESPOND TO THESE UNDERHANDED ATTACKS.

KIMBALL UNCOVERED A RECORDING OF A SPEECH McCAIN MADE TO UNIVERSITY STUDENTS MONTHS EARLIER. IN IT, HE DISCUSSED THE HIGH VOTER TURNOUT OF THE ELDERLY IN AN ARIZONA RETIREMENT COMMUNITY, MISPRONOUNCING "LEISURE WORLD" AS "SEIZURE WORLD" AND ADDING:

THE LAST ELECTION IN 1984, 97 PERCENT OF THE PEOPLE WHO LIVE THERE CAME OUT TO VOTE. I THINK THE OTHER 3 PERCENT WERE IN INTENSIVE CARE.

NEXT, KIMBALL TROTTED OUT SOME SPECIFICS OF McCAIN'S CAMPAIGN FINANCES. WHILE IT WAS ALREADY KNOWN THAT McCAIN WAS OUTSPENDING KIMBALL 4-1 IN THE RACE, KIMBALL ALLEGED HE WAS...

...BOUGHT AND PAID FOR BY A WHO'S WHO OF HIGH DOLLAR SPECIAL INTERESTS LOOKING FOR POLITICAL PROTECTION.

McCAIN, INCENSED BY KIMBALL AND WHAT HE CALLED "ONE OF THE MOST SLOPPY AND DIRTY CAMPAIGNS IN ARIZONA HISTORY," WAITED FOR THE TWO CANDIDATES' UPCOMING DEBATE TO EVEN THE SCORE.

BUT WHEN IT CAME, McCAIN SAW A PROBLEM. THE WAY TELEVISION CAMERAS WERE POSITIONED IN THE AUDITORIUM, McCAIN, ALREADY SIX INCHES SHORTER THAN HIS OPPONENT, WOULD SEEM, ACCORDING TO AN ADVISOR, "TO LOOK LIKE A PYGMY."

YOU COME IN HERE AND YOU TREAT PEOPLE FOR SUCKERS. YOU STAND ON A SOAPBOX TO MAKE YOURSELF APPEAR TO LOOK TALLER.

6ft

THE QUICK SOLUTION WAS TO HAVE McCAIN STAND ON A PLATFORM DISCREETLY PLACED BEHIND HIS PODIUM. BUT THIS TACTIC WAS EXPOSED BY KIMBALL AND USED AGAINST McCAIN DURING THE DEBATE:

AND EVEN AS THE SENATORIAL ELECTION MOVED TOWARDS ITS CLIMAX, McCAIN WAS CONFRONTED WITH PROBLEMS FROM A NEW SOURCE: NEWSPAPER PUBLISHER, POLITICAL MENTOR, AND CLOSE PERSONAL FRIEND "DUKE" TULLY WAS "CRACKING UP."

TULLY'S YEARS OF MILITARY SERVICE—STORIES WHICH HE HAD SHARED WITH McCAIN OVER THE YEARS—TURNED OUT TO HAVE BEEN ENTIRELY FICTIONALIZED. THE EXPOSURE OF THE SHAM HUMILIATED TULLY, FORCING HIM TO RESIGN.

THE ARIZONA Endorsement: McCain For Senate

McCAIN WON THE ELECTION, BUT LOST THE UNWAVERING SUPPORT OF ONE OF HIS STRONGEST BENEFACTORS; WITH TULLY'S FICTIONALIZED WAR STORIES EXPOSED, McCAIN AND OTHER FORMER FRIENDS DISTANCED THEMSELVES FROM THE DISGRACED PUBLISHER.

BUT AT THE START OF 1987, AT AGE 50, McCAIN WAS NOW A SENATOR—

—AND OUTGOING SENATOR BARRY GOLDWATER HIMSELF MADE CERTAIN McCAIN RECEIVED A PRIZED SEAT ON THE SENATE ARMED SERVICES COMMITTEE.

HIS NAME WAS NOW SPOKEN IN THE HIGHEST CORRIDORS OF POWER. THE ADMIRAL'S SON HAD ACHIEVED A RANK OF HIS OWN.

ON OCTOBER 8, 1989, HOWEVER, HIS SKIES DARKENED. WASHINGTON AND THE AMERICAN PEOPLE WOULD SOON BE PRESENTED WITH A VERY DIFFERENT IMAGE OF THEIR FRESHMAN SENATOR.

FACE THE NATION

ON THAT DAY, McCAIN SEEMED TO BE RIDING HIGH. HE APPEARED ON TV TO DISCUSS U.S. INVOLVEMENT IN PANAMA. HIS OP-ED PIECES AGAINST A CONTROVERSIAL HEALTH INSURANCE BILL RAN IN THE *WASHINTON POST* AND THE *L.A. TIMES.*

BUT IN PHOENIX, THE NEWLY ANTAGONISTIC *ARIZONA REPUBLIC* WAS REPORTING McCAIN'S QUESTIONABLE RELATIONSHIP WITH HIS OLD FRIEND CHARLES KEATING, WHOSE SAVINGS & LOAN EMPIRE WAS CRUMBLING.

BY 1987 McCAIN HAD RECEIVED OVER $110,000 IN POLITICAL CONTRIBUTIONS FOR HIS VARIOUS CAMPAIGNS FROM KEATING AND HIS ASSOCIATES. PERHAPS IN CONSIDERATION, A YEAR EARLIER McCAIN HAD CO-SPONSORED A HOUSE RESOLUTION TO DELAY INSTITUTING NEW RULES DESIGNED TO MAKE S & Ls LESS RISKY TO THE PUBLIC.

AND IN 1987, DEMOCRAT DENNIS DECONCINI, ARIZONA'S SENIOR SENATOR, CONVEYED A REQUEST FROM KEATING TO McCAIN. HE WANTED McCAIN AND OTHER SENATORS TO MEET WITH OFFICIALS OF THE FEDERAL HOME LOAN BANK BOARD.

KEATING NEEDED THE BOARD TO MAKE CERTAIN CONCESSIONS TO PROP UP HIS FAILING LINCOLN SAVINGS & LOAN AND WANTED HIS GOOD FRIEND McCAIN TO INTERVENE ON HIS BEHALF.

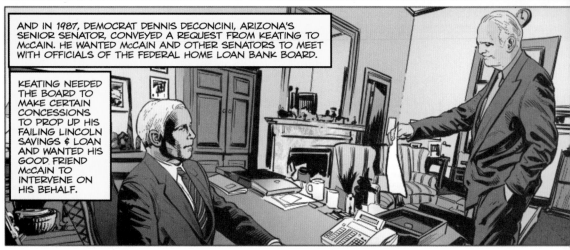

McCAIN REFUSED. BUT WHEN AN INSISTENT KEATING SHOWED UP IN McCAIN'S D.C. OFFICE, HE RELUCTANTLY AGREED TO ATTEND THE MEETINGS, IF ONLY TO ASCERTAIN WHETHER THE BANK REGULATORS WERE TREATING KEATING FAIRLY.

TWO MEETINGS WERE HELD IN EARLY APRIL 1987. BY THE SECOND MEETING, FIVE SENATORS—McCAIN, DECONCINI, CRANSTON OF CALIFORNIA, GLENN OF OHIO, AND DON RIEGLE OF MICHIGAN—ATTENDED.

THE SHOW OF SENATORS, McCAIN LATER CONCEDED, MIGHT HAVE IN ITSELF INTIMIDATED THE GROUP OF EXAMINERS, WHICH INCLUDED TOP LEVEL OFFICIALS OF THE FEDERAL HOME LOAN BANK BOARD AND THE FEDERAL SAVINGS AND LOAN INSURANCE CORP.

I DON'T WANT ANY PART OF OUR CONVERSATION TO BE IMPROPER...

...McCAIN BEGAN ONE OF THE MEETINGS, PERHAPS SENSING HE WAS TREADING ON SHAKY GROUND. BUT THE STATEMENT ONLY SERVED TO INTIMIDATE THE EXAMINERS. THEY VIEWED THE GROUP OF SENATORS AS BEING UNITED AGAINST THEM.

McCAIN REMAINED SILENT FOR THE REST OF THE MEETINGS, BUT A STATEMENT BY AN AUDITOR FROM THE FSLIC SHOOK THE SENATORS:

WE'RE SENDING A CRIMINAL REFERRAL TO THE DEPARTMENT OF JUSTICE. NOT MAYBE, WE'RE SENDING ONE.

THIS IS AN EXTRAORDINARILY SERIOUS MATTER. IT INVOLVES A WHOLE RANGE OF IMPRUDENT ACTIONS

WITH THAT, THE MEETING ENDED.

WORD OF THE SENATORS' ATTEMPT TO INFLUENCE THE AUDITORS SPREAD. THE GROUP, ALL OF WHOM HAD RECEIVED POLITICAL DONATIONS FROM KEATING, BECAME KNOWN AS "THE KEATING FIVE..."

AND WHEN LINCOLN FINALLY DECLARED BANKRUPTCY IN APRIL 1989, IT HAD LOST BILLIONS OF DOLLARS, MUCH OF IT THE SAVINGS OF ELDERLY INVESTORS, AND IT THREATENED TO TAKE THE CAREERS OF McCAIN AND THE OTHER SENATORS WITH IT.

DURING THE SENATE ETHICS COMMITTEE INVESTIGATION, IT WAS DISCOVERED THAT McCAIN AND HIS FAMILY HAD TAKEN TRIPS TO KEATING'S ESTATE IN THE BAHAMAS DURING 1984, 1985, AND 1986, ALL AT KEATINGS' EXPENSE.

McCAIN DENIED THIS, BUT HE AND HIS WIFE COULD NOT PRODUCE ALL THE RECIEPTS NEEDED TO PROVE THEY'D PAID FOR THE TRIPS THEMSELVES.

AND THEN THERE WAS THE MATTER OF THE FOUNTAIN SQUARE PROJECT, A PHOENIX SHOPPING CENTER BEING DEVELOPED BY ONE OF KEATING'S COMPANIES IN WHICH CINDY McCAIN AND HER FATHER WERE INVESTORS.

BUT McCAIN DEFUSED THIS POTENTIAL PROBLEM BY POINTING OUT THAT THE COUPLE FILED SEPARATE INCOME TAX RETURNS, AND CINDY AND HER FATHER HAD MADE THE INVESTMENT WITHOUT HIS PARTICIPATION.

WHILE THE ETHICS COMMITTEE FAILED TO FIND McCAIN GUILTY OF ANYTHING MORE DAMAGING THAN "POOR JUDGMENT," THE PRESSURE TOOK ITS TOLL. WITH HIS HONESTY AND INTEGRITY BROUGHT INTO QUESTION, McCAIN SEEMED DEMORALIZED AND HIS WIFE CINDY TEARFULLY ADMITTED...

I WATCHED JOHN JUST CRUMBLE.

PERHAPS UNABLE TO WITNESS HER HUSBAND'S PAIN, CINDY DEVOTED HERSELF TO CHARITABLE WORKS, SPECIFICALLY A RELIEF ORGANIZATION SHE'D FOUNDED CALLED "AMERICAN VOLUNTARY MEDICAL TEAM."

CINDY JOINED THE TEAM AS IT TRAVELED TO HOT SPOTS AROUND THE WORLD, PROVIDING MEDICAL AID TO PEOPLE IN NEED IN PLACES LIKE EL SALVADOR, BANGLADESH AND VIETNAM.

MEANWHILE, HER HUSBAND, NOT CONTENT TO SIMPLY PUT THE KEATING AFFAIR BEHIND HIM, DEVOTED HIMSELF TO SALVAGING HIS CAREER.

HE TRAVELED AROUND THE COUNTRY, DISCUSSING THE KEATING INCIDENT WHENEVER ASKED. THE PRESS BELIEVED HE WAS FORTHRIGHT, HONEST, AND ABOVE ALL, LIKEABLE.

WHEN THE GULF WAR BROKE OUT IN 1991, THE MEDIA ONCE AGAIN CALLED ON McCAIN AND HIS EXPERTISE IN FOREIGN AFFAIRS.

APPEARANCES ON TELEVISION AND RADIO GAVE McCAIN SOMETHING BESIDES HIS CONTROVERSIAL RECENT PAST TO TALK ABOUT, AND GAVE THE PUBLIC SOMETHING ELSE TO ASSOCIATE HIM WITH.

WAR IN IRAQ
OPERATION:
DESERT STORM

BY THE 1992 REELECTION CAMPAIGN, McCAIN'S COMEBACK WAS COMPLETE. IN A THREE-WAY RACE, HE CLINCHED HIS SECOND SENATORIAL TERM WITH 56 PERCENT OF THE VOTE. AFTER THE VOTES WERE COUNTED, McCAIN TOLD *THE ARIZONA REPUBLIC*:

I THINK THIS PUTS THE [KEATING] ISSUE BEHIND ME, YES, POLITICALLY.

ONLY ONE PAINFUL REMINDER WAS LEFT TO EMERGE.

CINDY McCAIN, IT WAS REVEALED BY THE McCAIN FAMILY IN 1994, WAS A RECOVERING PRESCRIPTION DRUG ADDICT.

HER DEPENDENCE ON THE PAIN RELIEVERS PERCOCET AND VICODIN BEGAN IN 1989, WHILE McCAIN WAS IN THE THICK OF THE KEATING SCANDAL. EMOTIONAL DISTRESS, AND PAIN FROM TWO BACK SURGERIES, CINDY LATER TOLD REPORTERS, LED TO HER ADDICTION.

I'M CINDY, AND I'M AN ADDICT

ADD TO THAT A SENSE OF PERSONAL RESPONSIBILITY FOR AT LEAST PART OF HER HUSBAND'S TROUBLES; AS THE FAMILY BOOKKEEPER, CINDY HAD MISPLACED THE AIR FARE RECEIPTS THAT WOULD HAVE PROVED THE FAMILY'S ANNUAL BAHAMA VACATIONS HAD BEEN PAID FOR BY McCAIN, NOT KEATING.

WHATEVER THE REASONS FOR CINDY McCAIN'S ADDICTION, THE CONSEQUENCES BECAME EVEN MORE DIRE WHEN IT WAS LEARNED SHE HAD FED HER HABIT WITH PILLS SHE'D TAKEN FROM THE RELIEF ORGANIZATION SHE'D FOUNDED.

THE D.E.A., ACTING ON A TIP FROM A DISGRUNTLED FORMER EMPLOYEE OF THE AMERICAN VOLUNTARY MEDICAL TEAM, AUDITED THE CHARITY'S DRUG SUPPLIES, AND WERE SOON AT THE McCAINS' DOOR.

RATHER THAN FACE CHARGES, CINDY ENTERED A FEDERAL DIVERSION PROGRAM. McCAIN, PREOCCUPIED WITH HIS OWN PROBLEMS, FAILED TO NOTICE HIS WIFE'S DEPENDENCY, BUT ONCE AWARE OF IT, SAID:

I'M VERY PROUD SHE WAS ABLE TO COME OUT OF IT.

FOR HER, IT WAS LIKE THE KEATING AFFAIR HAD BEEN FOR ME, A SEARING EXPERIENCE, AND WE BOTH CAME OUT STRONGER.

IN 1992 GEORGE H. W. BUSH WAS DEFEATED BY DEMOCRAT BILL CLINTON. McCAIN REACHED OUT TO SUPPORT HIS NEW PRESIDENT.

ALONG WITH SENATOR JOHN KERRY, THE TWO VIETNAM VETERANS SPEARHEADED CLINTON'S EFFORTS TO ESTABLISH DIPLOMATIC RELATIONS WITH VIETNAM, DESPITE PROTESTS FROM SOME OTHER VIETNAM VETS.

IN 1995 McCAIN REVERSED HIS STAND ON AMERICAN INVOLVEMENT IN THE BALKAN CONFLICT, OPPOSING OTHER REPUBLICANS WHO WANTED TO CUT OFF FUNDING FOR AMERICAN PEACEKEEPERS IN BOSNIA.

McCAIN VOTED IN FAVOR OF FUNDING BECAUSE "I KNOW WHAT IT MEANS WHEN TROOPS ARE PUT IN HARM'S WAY AND CONGRESS DOESN'T SUPPORT THEM."

ON THE DOMESTIC FRONT, McCAIN FOUGHT FOR THE "LINE-ITEM VETO," WHICH WOULD ALLOW A PRESIDENT TO ELIMINATE SELECT ITEMS OF A BILL WITHOUT VETOING THE ENTIRE BILL.

INTENDED TO CURB "PORK BARREL SPENDING" ITEMS, THE BILL PASSED IN 1996, BUT WAS RULED AS UNCONSTITUTIONAL BY THE SUPREME COURT TWO YEARS LATER.

ALONG THE SAME DOMESTIC REFORM LINES, IN 1996 McCAIN HELPED PUSH THROUGH MEASURES TO LIMIT THE TYPES AND AMOUNTS OF GIFTS MEMBERS OF CONGRESS AND THEIR FAMILIES COULD ACCEPT.

IT WAS AS IF, IN HIS SECOND TERM, McCAIN WAS CONFRONTING ALL THE NEGATIVES HE HIMSELF HAD BEEN ACCUSED OF, AND WAS ATTEMPTING TO SET THINGS RIGHT.

AND NOWHERE WAS THIS MORE EVIDENT THAN IN McCAIN'S EFFORTS ON BEHALF OF CAMPAIGN FINANCE REFORM. THE PROBLEM IN NEED OF REFORM WAS UNREGULATED "SOFT MONEY," DONATIONS MADE TO POLITICAL PARTIES AND USED TO FUND ATTACK ADS ON OPPOSITION CANDIDATES.

IN CONTRAST, "HARD MONEY" CONTRIBUTIONS WERE DIRECTED TO THE CANDIDATES THEMSELVES, AND THE AMOUNT OF INDIVIDUAL CONTRIBUTIONS WERE LIMITED, THE BETTER TO LEVEL THE FINANCIAL PLAYING FIELD.

BY THE MID '90s, "SOFT MONEY" CONTRIBUTIONS WERE SPIRALING OUT OF CONTROL, AND McCAIN AND WISCONSIN DEMOCRATIC SENATOR RUSS FEINGOLD JOINED FORCES IN WHAT THE TWO SAW AS A BIPARTISAN ATTEMPT TO OUTLAW A CORRUPTION-PRONE PROCESS.

BUT WHILE THE PRESS AND THE PUBLIC SEEMED TO LIKE THE McCAIN/FEINGOLD PLAN, NEITHER POLITICAL PARTY WAS PREPARED TO STEP UP IN SUPPORT.

JUST BEFORE ELECTION DAY 1996, CLINTON ANNOUNCED HIS SUPPORT FOR McCAIN/FEINGOLD, EVEN WHILE DEPENDING ON SOFT MONEY IN HIS OWN CAMPAIGN.

AFTER THE ELECTION, WHILE DEMOCRATS CONTINUED THEIR SUPPORT, REPUBLICANS REMAINED OPPOSED, SAYING A BAN WOULD BE AN INFRINGEMENT ON FREE SPEECH.

NOT UNTIL 2002 WOULD A DILUTED VERSION OF McCAIN/FEINGOLD, NOW REFERRED TO AS THE BIPARTISAN CAMPAIGN REFORM ACT, SQUEAK THROUGH THE SENATE WITH THE MINIMUM OF 60 VOTES NEEDED TO SHUT OFF DEBATE. WHEN PRESIDENT BUSH SIGNED THE ACT INTO LAW, HIS PRAISE WAS FAINT...

THIS LEGISLATION, ALTHOUGH FAR FROM PERFECT, WILL IMPROVE THE CURRENT FINANCING SYSTEM FOR FEDERAL CAMPAIGNS...

...TAKEN AS A WHOLE, THIS BILL IMPROVES THE CURRENT SYSTEM OF FINANCING...

BY THE LATE '90s, McCAIN WAS AT THE TOP OF HIS GAME. HE HAD BECOME ONE OF THE MOST VISIBLE SENATORS ON THE HILL, REGULARLY APPEARING ON THE SUNDAY MORNING TALK SHOWS AND CNN.

EQUAL PARTS POLITICIAN AND CELEBRITY, McCAIN PROFILES HAD MADE THE COVER OF *THE NEW YORK TIMES MAGAZINE* AND *USA TODAY. TIME MAGAZINE* NAMED HIM ONE OF THE 25 MOST INFLUENTIAL AMERICANS. HE WAS EVEN FEATURED IN AN EPISODE OF THE *BIOGRAPHY* TELEVISION SERIES.

IN AUGUST 1999, *FAITH OF MY FATHERS*, McCAIN'S FAMILY MEMOIR WAS PUBLISHED TO GLOWING REVIEWS. IN ADDITION TO BECOMING A BESTSELLER, IT WAS LATER ADAPTED INTO A MOVIE.

WITH CREDENTIALS LIKE THESE, IT CAME AS LITTLE SURPRISE WHEN, ON SEPTEMBER 27, 1999, JOHN McCAIN ANNOUNCED HE WAS RUNNING FOR PRESIDENT.

WORKING OUT OF A MOBILE CAMPAIGN HEADQUARTERS, A BUS HE DUBBED THE "STRAIGHT TALK EXPRESS," McCAIN USED HIS RAPPORT WITH THE MEDIA TO GOOD EFFECT, KEEPING THE BUS FILLED WITH REPORTERS WITH WHOM HE'D DISCUSS HIS CAMPAIGN POSITIONS OR JUST SHOOT THE BREEZE FOR HOURS ON END.

IT WAS DURING THOSE TIMES, WHEN McCAIN WAS LIKELY TO LET SLIP A SPONTANEOUS OFF-COLOR REMARK, THAT THE REPORTERS ESPECIALLY LIKED HIM.

WHEN NOT WORKING THE BUS, McCAIN WOULD USUALLY BE SURROUNDED BY ORDINARY VOTERS WHO ATTENDED HIS TOWN HALL MEETINGS. McCAIN SEEMED INEXHAUSTIBLE AT THESE EVENTS, REFUSING TO LEAVE THE STAGE UNTIL HE'D ANSWERED EVERY VOTER'S QUESTION.

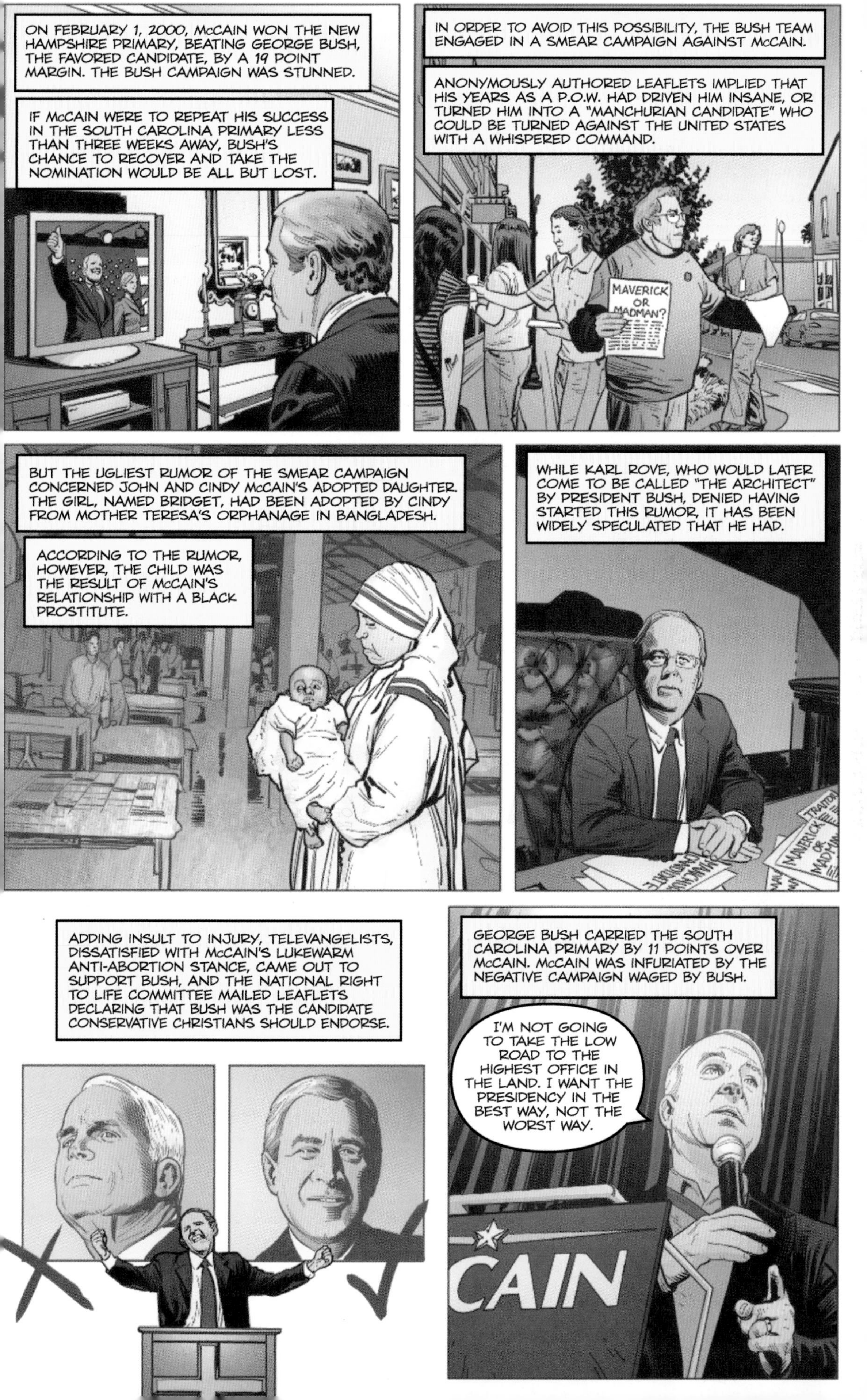
ON FEBRUARY 1, 2000, McCAIN WON THE NEW HAMPSHIRE PRIMARY, BEATING GEORGE BUSH, THE FAVORED CANDIDATE, BY A 19 POINT MARGIN. THE BUSH CAMPAIGN WAS STUNNED.
IF McCAIN WERE TO REPEAT HIS SUCCESS IN THE SOUTH CAROLINA PRIMARY LESS THAN THREE WEEKS AWAY, BUSH'S CHANCE TO RECOVER AND TAKE THE NOMINATION WOULD BE ALL BUT LOST.
IN ORDER TO AVOID THIS POSSIBILITY, THE BUSH TEAM ENGAGED IN A SMEAR CAMPAIGN AGAINST McCAIN.
ANONYMOUSLY AUTHORED LEAFLETS IMPLIED THAT HIS YEARS AS A P.O.W. HAD DRIVEN HIM INSANE, OR TURNED HIM INTO A "MANCHURIAN CANDIDATE" WHO COULD BE TURNED AGAINST THE UNITED STATES WITH A WHISPERED COMMAND.
MAVERICK OR MADMAN?
BUT THE UGLIEST RUMOR OF THE SMEAR CAMPAIGN CONCERNED JOHN AND CINDY McCAIN'S ADOPTED DAUGHTER. THE GIRL, NAMED BRIDGET, HAD BEEN ADOPTED BY CINDY FROM MOTHER TERESA'S ORPHANAGE IN BANGLADESH.
ACCORDING TO THE RUMOR, HOWEVER, THE CHILD WAS THE RESULT OF McCAIN'S RELATIONSHIP WITH A BLACK PROSTITUTE.
WHILE KARL ROVE, WHO WOULD LATER COME TO BE CALLED "THE ARCHITECT" BY PRESIDENT BUSH, DENIED HAVING STARTED THIS RUMOR, IT HAS BEEN WIDELY SPECULATED THAT HE HAD.
TRAITOR
MAVERICK OR MADMAN
ADDING INSULT TO INJURY, TELEVANGELISTS, DISSATISFIED WITH McCAIN'S LUKEWARM ANTI-ABORTION STANCE, CAME OUT TO SUPPORT BUSH, AND THE NATIONAL RIGHT TO LIFE COMMITTEE MAILED LEAFLETS DECLARING THAT BUSH WAS THE CANDIDATE CONSERVATIVE CHRISTIANS SHOULD ENDORSE.
GEORGE BUSH CARRIED THE SOUTH CAROLINA PRIMARY BY 11 POINTS OVER McCAIN. McCAIN WAS INFURIATED BY THE NEGATIVE CAMPAIGN WAGED BY BUSH.
I'M NOT GOING TO TAKE THE LOW ROAD TO THE HIGHEST OFFICE IN THE LAND. I WANT THE PRESIDENCY IN THE BEST WAY, NOT THE WORST WAY.
CAIN

DESPITE HIS DEFEAT IN SOUTH CAROLINA, McCAIN WON THE NEXT TWO PRIMARIES IN ARIZONA AND MICHIGAN. BUT THE FOLLOWING WEEK, ON FEBRUARY 28, McCAIN RESPONDED TO ATTACKS MADE ON HIM BY THE RELIGIOUS RIGHT.

NEITHER PARTY SHOULD BE DEFINED BY PANDERING TO THE OUTER REACHES OF AMERICAN POLITICS AND THE AGENTS OF INTOLERANCE, WHETHER THEY BE LOUIS FARRAKHAN OR AL SHARPTON ON THE LEFT, OR PAT ROBERTSON OR JERRY FALWELL ON THE RIGHT.

BY ATTACKING THE RELIGIOUS AND SOCIAL CONSERVATIVES, McCAIN HAD EFFECTIVELY HANDED THEIR SUPPORT OVER TO BUSH.

ON MARCH 7TH, SUPER TUESDAY, BUSH CARRIED 9 OF THE 13 PRIMARIES.

McCAIN'S RUN FOR THE WHITE HOUSE WAS OVER.

WHEN, IN AUGUST 2000, GEORGE BUSH ACCEPTED THE REPUBLICAN NOMINATION FOR PRESIDENT, McCAIN WAS THERE TO CONGRATULATE HIM, AND TO REMARK: "I SUPPORT HIM, I AM GRATEFUL TO HIM. AND I AM PROUD OF HIM."

SHORTLY AFTERWARD, McCAIN WAS IN THE HOSPITAL, UNDERGOING SURGERY FOR A SECOND TIME TO REMOVE CARCINOGENIC MELANOMAS FROM HIS ARMS AND FACE, LEAVING HIM WITH A NOTICEABLE SCAR.

McCAIN WAS BACK AT WORK IN TIME TO DO SOME HALFHEARTED STUMPING FOR NOMINEE BUSH. BUT ONCE THE WINNER OF THE ELECTION HAD BEEN DECIDED, McCAIN RETURNED TO THE SENATE, AND RETURNED TO HIS INDEPENDENT, BI-PARTISAN MINDED WAYS.

IN FEBRUARY HE DEFIED BUSH'S WISHES BY JOINING SENATORS EDWARD KENNEDY AND JOHN EDWARDS ON A HMO REFORM BILL.

IN MAY, HE SPOKE OUT AGAINST BUSH'S REJECTION OF THE KYOTO PROTOCOL CLIMATE CONTROL TREATY, AND LATER THAT MONTH, ATTEMPTED TO INTRODUCE LEGISLATION TO INCREASE REGULATION OF GUN SALES AT GUN SHOWS.

AND MOST AUDACIOUSLY, ON MAY 27 HIS WAS ONE OF ONLY TWO REPUBLICAN VOTES AGAINST BUSH'S TRILLION DOLLAR TAX RELIEF PACKAGE, BECAUSE, ACCORDING TO McCAIN, THE CUTS BENEFITED THE WEALTHY AND NOT THE MIDDLE CLASS.

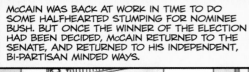

THE ADVERSARIAL RELATIONSHIP BETWEEN BUSH AND McCAIN WAS SUDDENLY SET ASIDE AFTER THE EVENTS OF SEPTEMBER 11, 2001. AS THE PRESIDENT WAS NOW A WAR-TIME COMMANDER-IN-CHIEF, McCAIN FELT COMPELLED TO OFFER HIS SUPPORT.

BUT McCAIN'S DIFFERING OPINIONS ABOUT THE PARTICULARS OF BUSH'S AIR-BASED BATTLE STRATEGY IN AFGHANISTAN WENT LARGELY IGNORED, RESULTING, SOME BELIEVE, IN OSAMA BIN LADEN'S ESCAPE DURING THE BATTLE OF TORA BORA.

STILL, WHILE THE BUSH ADMINISTRATION PAID McCAIN LITTLE HEED, THE MEDIA ONCE AGAIN FLOCKED TO HIM FOR HIS OPINIONS ON HOW THE AMERICAN MILITARY COULD BEST CONDUCT ITS WAR ON TERRORISM.

SENSING CERTAIN PARALLELS TO VIETNAM, McCAIN COULD OFFER NO EASY SOLUTIONS. INSTEAD, HE SAID:

WAR IS A MISERABLE BUSINESS. LET'S GET ON WITH IT.

IN OCTOBER, McCAIN AND DEMOCRATIC SENATOR ERNEST HOLLINGS SPONSORED A BILL TO CREATE THE TRANSPORTATION SECURITY ADMINISTRATION, WHICH PLACED ALL AIRLINE SECURITY UNDER FEDERAL CONTROL.

THE 9/11 COMMISSION REPORT

REPORT OF THE NATIONAL COMMISSION ON ATTACKS UPON THE UNITED STATES

AND THAT DECEMBER, McCAIN AND DEMOCRATIC SENATOR JOSEPH LIEBERMAN PRESENTED A BILL TO EXAMINE THE EVENTS LEADING UP TO THE TERRORIST ATTACKS. BOTH BIPARTISAN BILLS WON SWEEPING APPROVAL.

ONCE THE TALIBAN FLED AFGHANISTAN, THE BUSH ADMINISTRATION SET ITS SIGHTS ON SADDAM HUSSEIN. McCAIN STOOD SOLIDLY BEHIND THE PRESIDENT, CALLING HUSSEIN:

A MEGALOMANIACAL TYRANT WHOSE CRUELTY AND OFFENSE TO THE NORMS OF CIVILIZATION ARE INFAMOUS.

HE VOTED IN FAVOR OF THE IRAQ WAR RESOLUTION, WHICH READIED THE STAGE FOR WAR IN MARCH 2003.

WHILE McCAIN INITIALLY SHARED THE ADMINISTRATION'S BELIEF THAT THE IRAQI PEOPLE WOULD WELCOME THE AMERICAN FORCES AS LIBERATORS, THEY HAD UNDERESTIMATED THE TRIBAL AND RELIGIOUS HOSTILITY THAT HUSSEIN HAD LONG SUPPRESSED.

IRAN

WITH AMERICAN FORCES COMING UNDER ATTACK FROM ALL SIDES, McCAIN TRAVELED TO IRAQ TO ASSESS THE SITUATION. HE RETURNED WITH THE BELIEF THAT THE WAR EFFORT WAS FATALLY FLAWED.

FOR THIS, HE HELD SECRETARY OF DEFENSE DONALD RUMSFELD RESPONSIBLE. THE SUBSEQUENT DISCOVERY OF THE ADMINISTRATIONS USE OF "ENHANCED INTERROGATION TECHNIQUES" ON PRISONERS LED McCAIN TO INTRODUCE A BILL TO PROHIBIT ACTIONS THAT COULD BE CONSIDERED TORTURE.

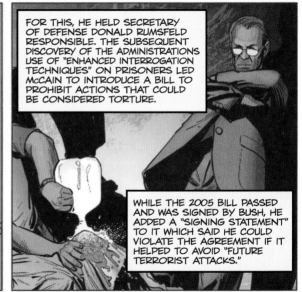

WHILE THE 2005 BILL PASSED AND WAS SIGNED BY BUSH, HE ADDED A "SIGNING STATEMENT" TO IT WHICH SAID HE COULD VIOLATE THE AGREEMENT IF IT HELPED TO AVOID "FUTURE TERRORIST ATTACKS."

IN 2006 McCAIN GAVE THE COMMENCEMENT ADDRESS AT JERRY FALWELL'S LIBERTY UNIVERSITY, A TURNAROUND FOR McCAIN, WHO ONCE CALLED FALWELL ONE OF THE "AGENTS OF INTOLERANCE."

HE ALSO VOTED IN FAVOR OF BUSH'S TAX CUT EXTENSION, A BILL HE PREVIOUSLY SAID BENEFITED THE RICH AT THE EXPENSE OF THE POOR.

IT SEEMED TO MANY THAT THE "MAVERICK" WAS GOING "ESTABLISHMENT," SUDDENLY FORSAKING HIS INDEPENDENT SPIRIT AND TOEING THE REPUBLICAN LINE.

ON FEBRUARY 28, 2007, ON THE DAVID LETTERMAN SHOW, McCAIN ANNOUNCED HE WOULD SEEK THE REPUBLICAN NOMINATION FOR PRESIDENT.

BUT DESPITE BEING THE MOST RECOGNIZABLE CANDIDATE, BY JULY HE HAD ALL BUT RUN OUT OF CAMPAIGN FUNDS. IT SEEMED HE WOULD BE FORCED TO DROP OUT—UNTIL AN UPSET WIN IN THE NEW HAMPSHIRE PRIMARY ON JANUARY 8, 2008, BEGAN TURNING HIS LUCK AROUND.

OTHER CANDIDATES, SUCH AS FRONT-RUNNERS RUDY GIULIANI AND MITT ROMNEY, STARTED TO ATTRACT CONTROVERSY AND VOTER UNCERTAINTY FOR THEIR POLITICAL, SOCIAL, AND RELIGIOUS CONVICTIONS. THIS CLEARED THE WAY FOR McCAIN TO PULL AWAY FROM THE PACK.

PRO-ABORTION!

MORMON!

LITTLE MORE THAN A MONTH LATER, A STRING OF PRIMARY WINS FROM ACROSS THE NATION SECURED McCAIN'S PLACE AS THE PRESUMPTIVE REPUBLICAN CANDIDATE FOR PRESIDENT OF THE UNITED STATES.

WITH THE CHALLENGE FROM WITHIN HIS PARTY BEHIND HIM, JOHN McCAIN SET HIS SIGHTS ON OVERCOMING PERHAPS HIS MOST FORMIDABLE ADVERSARY...

...DEMOCRATIC PRESUMPTIVE CANDIDATE BARACK OBAMA.

AND MAY THE BEST MAN WIN.

Written by Andy Helfer

Art by Stephen Thompson

Color by Len O'Grady

Letters by Robbie Robbins

Cover art by J. Scott Campbell

Cover color by Edgar Delgado

Edited by Scott Dunbier

The cover pencils by artist J. Scott Campbell

The final art by Campbell. Colors provided by Edgar Delgado.

Biographical sources for
Presidential Material: John McCain

Associated Press

Arizona Republic

Citizen McCain by Elizabeth Drew

CNN

Economist

Faith of my Fathers by John McCain

John McCain: An American Odyssey by Robert Timberg

Man of the People: The Life of John McCain by Paul Alexander

Newsweek

New Yorker

New York Times

New York Times Magazine

Salon.com

Senate.gov

The Real McCain by Cliff Schecter

Time

USA Today

U.S. News & World Report

Wall Street Journal

Worth the Fighting For by John McCain

Biographical sources for
Presidential Material: Barack Obama

ABC News
Boston Globe
Chicago Magazine
Chicago Sun-Times
Chicago Tribune
CNN
Foxnews.com
International Herald Tribune
MSNBC.com
New York Daily News
New York Times
New York Times Magazine
Senate.gov
Time
USA Today
Washington Post

Conversations portrayed on
pages 2, 3, 5, 6, 8, 10, 12 are quoted from
Dreams From My Father by Barack Obama

Conversations portrayed
on pages 17, 19, 21 are quoted from
The Audacity of Hope by Barack Obama

The final art by Campbell. Colors provided by Edgar Delgado.

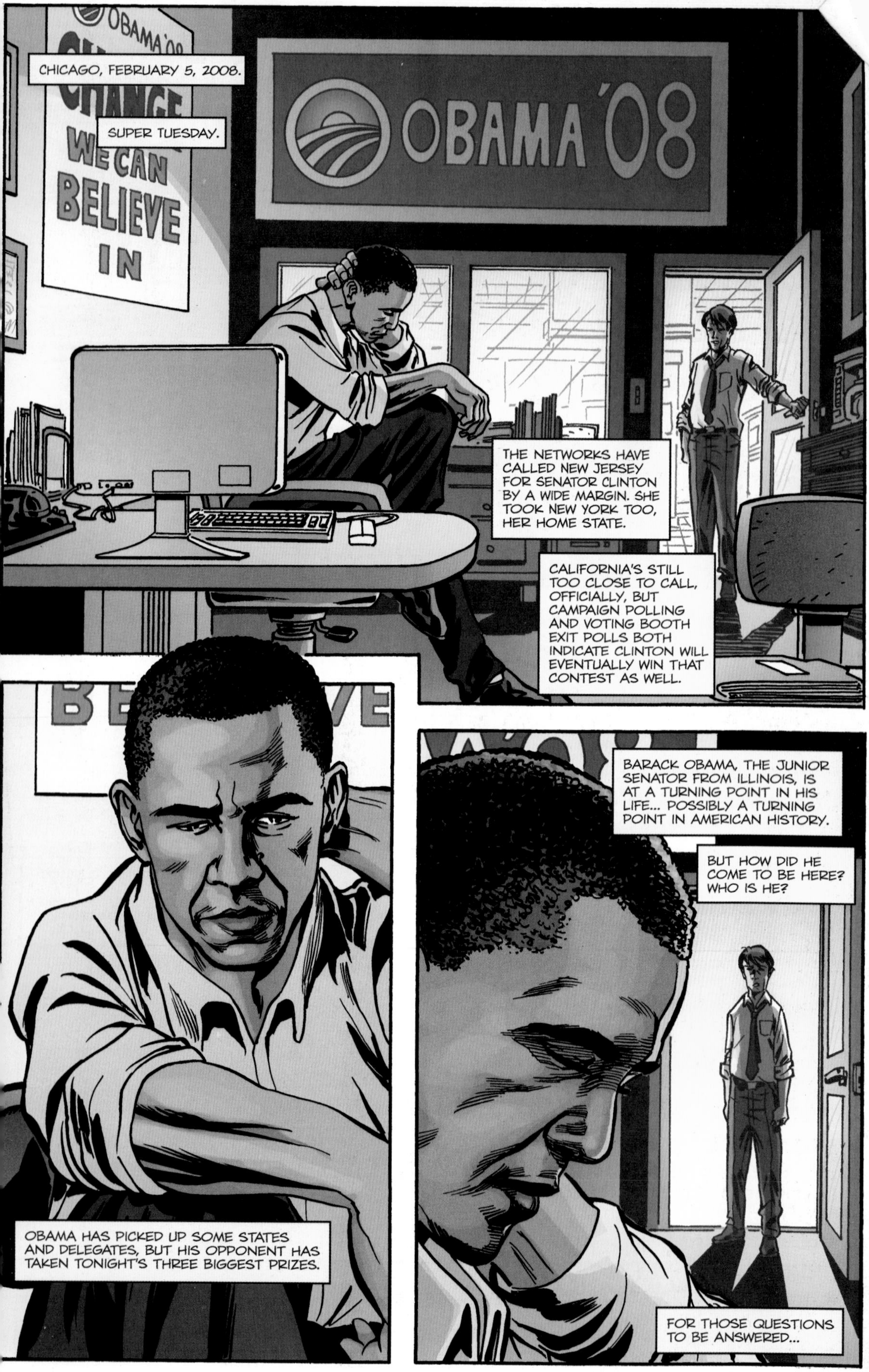
CHICAGO, FEBRUARY 5, 2008.
SUPER TUESDAY.
OBAMA '08
CHANGE WE CAN BELIEVE IN
THE NETWORKS HAVE CALLED NEW JERSEY FOR SENATOR CLINTON BY A WIDE MARGIN. SHE TOOK NEW YORK TOO, HER HOME STATE.
CALIFORNIA'S STILL TOO CLOSE TO CALL, OFFICIALLY, BUT CAMPAIGN POLLING AND VOTING BOOTH EXIT POLLS BOTH INDICATE CLINTON WILL EVENTUALLY WIN THAT CONTEST AS WELL.
OBAMA HAS PICKED UP SOME STATES AND DELEGATES, BUT HIS OPPONENT HAS TAKEN TONIGHT'S THREE BIGGEST PRIZES.
BARACK OBAMA, THE JUNIOR SENATOR FROM ILLINOIS, IS AT A TURNING POINT IN HIS LIFE... POSSIBLY A TURNING POINT IN AMERICAN HISTORY.
BUT HOW DID HE COME TO BE HERE? WHO IS HE?
FOR THOSE QUESTIONS TO BE ANSWERED...

...WE NEED TO MOVE TO ANOTHER TIME AND PLACE, TO HAWAII, WHERE BARACK OBAMA WAS BORN, ON AUGUST 4, 1961. HIS NAME, BARACK, WAS ALSO HIS FATHER'S, AND MEANS "BLESSED."

IN MANY WAYS, HAWAII SEEMED LIKE AN IDYLLIC PLACE TO BE A BOY.

THERE WERE OCCASIONAL INCIDENTS, LIKE THIS EXCHANGE OBAMA RELATES IN *DREAMS FROM MY FATHER*, BETWEEN HIS GRANDFATHER AND A TOURIST:

SWIMMING MUST JUST COME NATURALLY TO THESE HAWAIIANS.

THAT BOY HAPPENS TO BE MY GRANDSON, HIS MOTHER IS FROM KANSAS, HIS FATHER IS FROM THE INTERIOR OF KENYA, AND THERE ISN'T AN OCEAN FOR MILES IN EITHER DAMN PLACE.

FROM HIS YOUNGEST DAYS, BARRY, THE NAME HE WENT BY AS A CHILD, NEVER QUITE FIT IN ANYWHERE. MIXED-RACE CHILDREN WERE RARE IN THE EARLY 1960s, EVEN IN HAWAII.

HIS MOTHER, STANLEY ANN DUNHAM—HER FATHER WANTED A BOY—HAD MOVED TO HAWAII IN 1959 OR 1960 (ACCOUNTS VARY), WITH HER PARENTS.

AT 18, ENROLLED IN A RUSSIAN LANGUAGE COURSE, SHE MET BARACK OBAMA, THE UNIVERSITY OF HAWAII'S FIRST AFRICAN STUDENT. THEY FELL IN LOVE, MARRIED, AND HAD A SON...

...BUT IN 1963, THE SENIOR OBAMA WENT TO HARVARD, EVENTUALLY EARNING A MASTERS DEGREE IN ECONOMICS, AFTER WHICH HE RETURNED TO KENYA. ALONE.

AFTER HER DIVORCE, ANN DUNHAM MET AN INDONESIAN STUDENT NAMED LOLO SOETORO AT THE EAST-WEST CENTER AT THE UNIVERSITY OF HAWAII.

IN 1967 THE COUPLE MARRIED AND SHORTLY THEREAFTER DUNHAM AND THE YOUNG OBAMA MOVED TO JAKARTA TO BE WITH HIM.

SOETORO WAS PLEASED TO BE REUNITED WITH HIS NEW FAMILY AFTER SEVERAL MONTHS APART.

ANN WONDERED WHY THE SOLDIERS WEREN'T CHECKING THEIR BAGS, TO WHICH HER HUSBAND REPLIED:

DON'T WORRY... THAT'S BEEN ALL TAKEN CARE OF. THOSE ARE FRIENDS OF MINE.

YOUNG BARRY, OF COURSE, DIDN'T KNOW INDONESIA'S HISTORY—AS A COLONY OF THE NETHERLANDS, FOLLOWED BY INDEPENDENCE AND THE ELECTION OF THEIR FIRST PRESIDENT, SUKARNO, IN 1945—OR THE RECENT MILITARY COUP THAT DEPOSED HIM.

THE CIA-BACKED PURGE HAD TAKEN HUNDREDS OF THOUSANDS OF LIVES—A CAMPAIGN OF SWIFT AND BRUTAL SUPPRESSION THAT LEFT THE COUNTRY IN SHOCK, AND BROUGHT GENERAL SUHARTO TO THE FOREFRONT AS INDONESIA'S SECOND PRESIDENT.

AND ANN, WHO HAD LOOKED FORWARD TO HELPING HER HUSBAND REBUILD HIS COUNTRY THROUGH HIS GOVERNMENT JOB, DIDN'T KNOW HOW ITS POLITICAL CHANGES HAD AFFECTED SOETORO, MAKING HIM WITHDRAWN, UNWILLING OR UNABLE TO COMMUNICATE.

LATER, WORKING FOR AN AMERICAN OIL COMPANY, SOETORO'S FORTUNES IMPROVED. HE WAS ABLE TO AFFORD A NICER HOUSE, A CAR, TO SIGN FOR MEALS AT THE COMPANY CLUB.

SOME OF HER HUSBAND'S PRACTICES DISTURBED ANN, LIKE HIDING THE REFRIGERATOR WHEN TAX OFFICIALS CAME SO THEY WOULDN'T SEE HOW WELL HE WAS DOING.

INDONESIA WAS AN IMPOVERISHED COUNTRY, AND HE DIDN'T WANT PEOPLE TO KNOW HE MADE ENOUGH MONEY TO AFFORD SUCH LUXURIES.

HE INSISTED THAT EVERYONE EXPECTED IT, EVEN THE TAX OFFICIALS. BUT THAT DIDN'T MAKE IT RIGHT TO HIS WIFE.

SHE WANTED HER SON TO KNOW THAT HONESTY WAS IMPORTANT. HIS FATHER WAS AN HONEST MAN. HONESTY, FAIRNESS, STRAIGHT TALK, INDEPENDENT JUDGMENT—THESE WERE CRUCIAL TRAITS FOR A MAN TO HAVE.

LITTLE MAYA, OBAMA'S BABY SISTER BORN IN 1970, NEEDED TO GROW UP WITH AN HONORABLE BIG BROTHER.

YOUNG BARRY'S EDUCATION CAME FROM EVERY DIRECTION AT ONCE—FROM 1967 TO 1970 HE ATTENDED FRANSISKUS STRADA ASISIA, A CATHOLIC SCHOOL, FOLLOWED BY TWO YEARS AT PUBLIC ELEMENTARY SCHOOL MENTENG NO. 1, A PREDOMINANTLY MUSLIM SCHOOL, AS WELL AS CORRESPONDENCE COURSES, THE STREETS, HIS MOTHER'S LESSONS AND THE BOOKS AND RECORDS ABOUT THE CIVIL RIGHTS MOVEMENT SHE GAVE HIM.

ONCE AGAIN, HE WAS UNIQUE, DIFFERENT FROM THOSE AROUND HIM.

MARTIN LUTHER KING JR. SPEAKS!

HIS MOTHER TRIED TO TEACH HIM TO EMBRACE THAT DIFFERENCE, AS WELL AS THE AFRICAN SIDE OF HIS HERITAGE, EVEN THOUGH HE HAD NO ROLE MODEL FOR THAT.

INSIDE THE CLASSROOM, THERE WERE SNICKERS WHEN THE TEACHER CALLED OUT THE NAME BARACK OBAMA.

YOUR GRANDFATHER'S FUNNY.

YEAH, HE IS.

HI THERE, THIS HERE'S BARRY, I'M BARRY'S GRANDFATHER, YOU CAN CALL ME GRAMPS, BARRY'S NEW.

ME TOO.

OBAMA, IN DREAMS FROM MY FATHER, RECALLED HIS FIRST DAY OF SCHOOL:

HE APPLIED TO, AND WAS ACCEPTED BY, THE PRESTIGIOUS PUNAHOU ACADEMY.

OBAMA'S MOTHER DECIDED HE WOULD BE BETTER OFF IN AN AMERICAN SCHOOL, SO SHE SENT HIM BACK TO HAWAII TO LIVE WITH HER PARENTS, STANLEY AND MADELYN DUNHAM, WHOM HE CALLED TOOT AND GRAMPS.

I THOUGHT YOUR NAME WAS BARRY.

WOULD YOU PREFER IF WE CALL YOU BARRY? BARACK IS SUCH A BEAUTIFUL NAME. YOUR GRANDFATHER TELLS ME YOUR FATHER IS KENYAN.

I USED TO LIVE IN KENYA, YOU KNOW. TEACHING CHILDREN JUST YOUR AGE. IT'S SUCH A MAGNIFICENT COUNTRY. DO YOU KNOW WHAT TRIBE YOUR FATHER IS FROM?

HA HA HA HA HA HA HA HA HA HA HA HA HA HA

LUO.

THE NAME PROMPTED MORE LAUGHTER.

ONE GIRL ASKED IF SHE COULD TOUCH BARACK'S HAIR, WHILE A BOY ASKED IF IT WAS TRUE THAT HIS FATHER ATE PEOPLE.

AFTER SCHOOL...

SO HOW WAS IT? ISN'T IT TERRIFIC THAT MISS HEFTY USED TO LIVE IN KENYA? MAKES THE FIRST DAY A LITTLE EASIER, I'LL BET.

SEPARATED FROM SOETORO, OBAMA'S MOTHER AND SISTER RETURNED TO HAWAII IN 1972, WHERE HIS MOTHER PURSUED A MASTER'S DEGREE. OBAMA, 11, LIVED WITH THEM FOR THREE YEARS, UNTIL SHE RETURNED TO INDONESIA TO DO ANTHROPOLOGICAL FIELDWORK. SHE WOULD EARN A PHD IN ANTHROPOLOGY IN 1992.

CHOOSING TO STAY BEHIND, OBAMA AGAIN LIVED WITH TOOT AND GRAMPS. HE SEARCHED FOR HIS IDENTITY, TRYING TO LEARN WHAT IT MEANT TO BE A BLACK MAN IN AN AMERICA CHANGING AS FAST AS HE WAS.

EVEN ON HIS HIGH SCHOOL BASKETBALL TEAM, AT PUNAHOU ACADEMY, HE FELT HE WAS IN THE WHITE MAN'S WORLD. BUT PLAYING WITH OLDER FRIENDS ON THE NEARBY UNIVERSITY COURTS, HE WAS FREE TO BE HIMSELF.

HE SOUGHT OUT THE COMPANY OF OTHER BLACK MEN, READ ELLISON, BALDWIN, HUGHES, WRIGHT, DUBOIS, AND MALCOLM X, AND TRIED TO FIGURE OUT WHERE HE BELONGED. HE WAS EXPERIMENTING WITH TOBACCO, ALCOHOL, POT, AND COCAINE.

"THINGS HAD GOTTEN COMPLICATED," OBAMA LATER WROTE, REFERRING TO THAT PERIOD IN HIS LIFE.

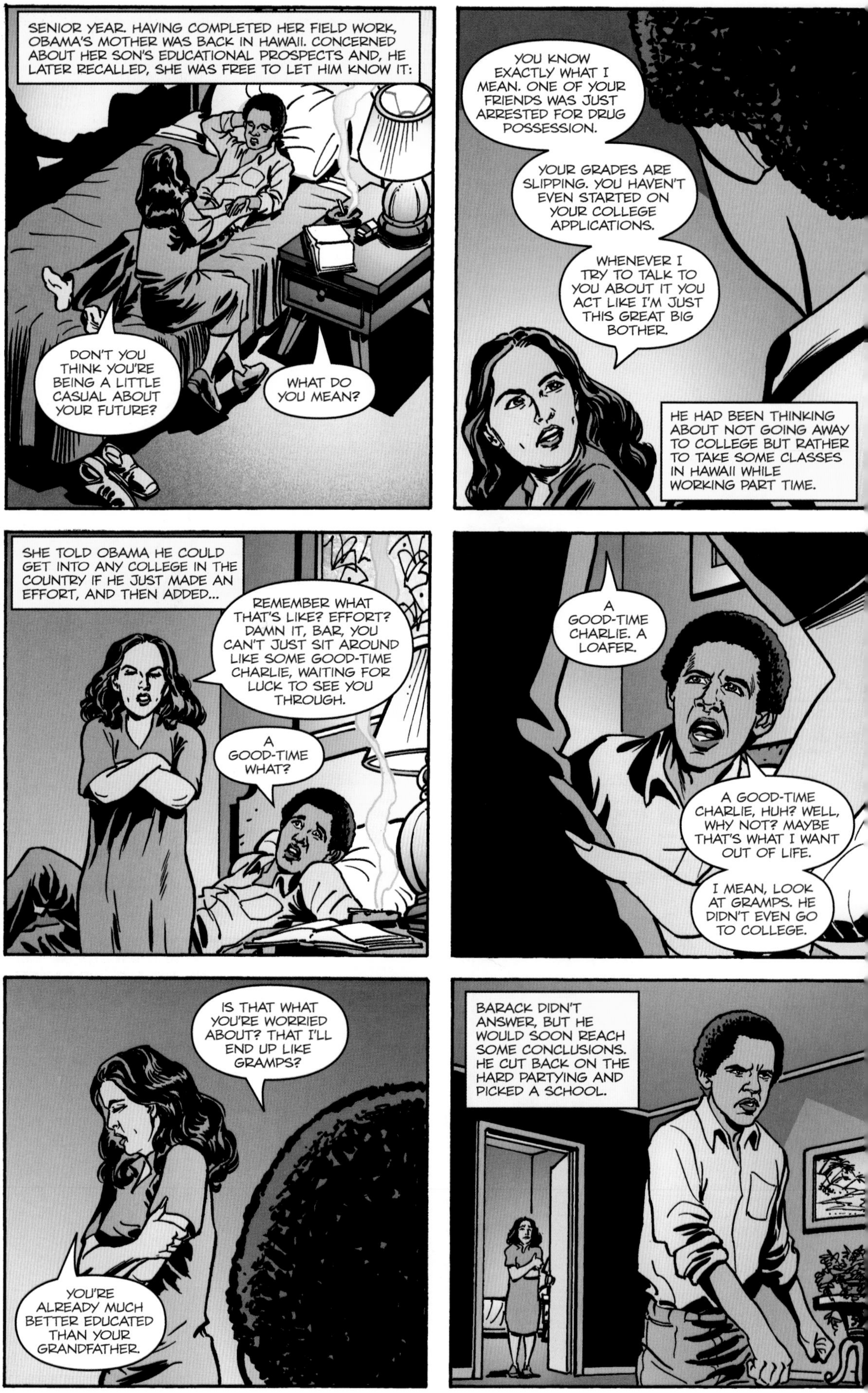
SENIOR YEAR. HAVING COMPLETED HER FIELD WORK, OBAMA'S MOTHER WAS BACK IN HAWAII. CONCERNED ABOUT HER SON'S EDUCATIONAL PROSPECTS AND, HE LATER RECALLED, SHE WAS FREE TO LET HIM KNOW IT:
DON'T YOU THINK YOU'RE BEING A LITTLE CASUAL ABOUT YOUR FUTURE?
WHAT DO YOU MEAN?
YOU KNOW EXACTLY WHAT I MEAN. ONE OF YOUR FRIENDS WAS JUST ARRESTED FOR DRUG POSSESSION.
YOUR GRADES ARE SLIPPING. YOU HAVEN'T EVEN STARTED ON YOUR COLLEGE APPLICATIONS.
WHENEVER I TRY TO TALK TO YOU ABOUT IT YOU ACT LIKE I'M JUST THIS GREAT BIG BOTHER.
HE HAD BEEN THINKING ABOUT NOT GOING AWAY TO COLLEGE BUT RATHER TO TAKE SOME CLASSES IN HAWAII WHILE WORKING PART TIME.
SHE TOLD OBAMA HE COULD GET INTO ANY COLLEGE IN THE COUNTRY IF HE JUST MADE AN EFFORT, AND THEN ADDED...
REMEMBER WHAT THAT'S LIKE? EFFORT? DAMN IT, BAR, YOU CAN'T JUST SIT AROUND LIKE SOME GOOD-TIME CHARLIE, WAITING FOR LUCK TO SEE YOU THROUGH.
A GOOD-TIME WHAT?
A GOOD-TIME CHARLIE. A LOAFER.
A GOOD-TIME CHARLIE, HUH? WELL, WHY NOT? MAYBE THAT'S WHAT I WANT OUT OF LIFE.
I MEAN, LOOK AT GRAMPS. HE DIDN'T EVEN GO TO COLLEGE.
IS THAT WHAT YOU'RE WORRIED ABOUT? THAT I'LL END UP LIKE GRAMPS?
YOU'RE ALREADY MUCH BETTER EDUCATED THAN YOUR GRANDFATHER.
BARACK DIDN'T ANSWER, BUT HE WOULD SOON REACH SOME CONCLUSIONS. HE CUT BACK ON THE HARD PARTYING AND PICKED A SCHOOL.

OCCIDENTAL COLLEGE, LOS ANGELES.

SOME OF HIS NEW FRIENDS PERSUADED HIM TO RETURN TO HIS GIVEN NAME—BARACK, NOT BARRY. DURING CHRISTMAS BREAK IN 1980, BACK IN HAWAII, HE TOLD HIS FAMILY. IT WAS A DECISION HE NEVER WENT BACK ON.

THERE HE BECAME FRIENDS WITH OTHER MULTIRACIAL STUDENTS... SOME OF WHOM RESENTED BEING CALLED BLACK, AND DIDN'T WANT TO HAVE TO CHOOSE ONE PART OF THEIR RACIAL HERITAGE OVER OTHERS SIMPLY BECAUSE OF THEIR SKIN COLOR.

ONE FRIEND, OBAMA RECALLED, DID NOT BELIEVE WHITE PEOPLE WANTED HER TO PICK A SINGLE RACE AND LIVE WITH THAT AS A FINAL DECISION, BUT SHE FELT BLACK PEOPLE PUSHED HER IN THAT DIRECTION.

BARACK LATER WROTE, "I CHOSE MY FRIENDS CAREFULLY. THE MORE POLITICALLY ACTIVE BLACK STUDENTS. THE FOREIGN STUDENTS. THE CHICANOS.

"THE MARXIST PROFESSORS AND STRUCTURAL FEMINISTS AND PUNK-ROCK PERFORMANCE POETS.

"WE SMOKED CIGARETTES AND WORE LEATHER JACKETS. AT NIGHT, IN THE DORMS, WE DISCUSSED NEOCOLONIALISM, FRANTZ FANON, EUROCENTRISM, AND PATRIARCHY.

"WHEN WE GROUND OUT OUR CIGARETTES IN THE HALLWAY CARPET OR SET OUR STEREOS SO LOUD THAT THE WALLS BEGAN TO SHAKE, WE WERE RESISTING BOURGEOIS SOCIETY'S STIFLING CONSTRAINTS.

"WE WEREN'T INDIFFERENT OR CARELESS OR INSECURE. WE WERE ALIENATED."

ON THE THEORY THAT COLUMBIA UNIVERSITY WOULD HAVE A LARGER BLACK POPULATION— OR FAILING THAT, NEW YORK WOULD HAVE BLACK NEIGHBORHOODS—BARACK TRANSFERRED THERE.

AFTER GRADUATING IN 1983 WITH A B.A., HE FOUND HIMSELF WORKING AS A FINANCIAL WRITER FOR BUSINESS INTERNATIONAL CORPORATION, A CONSULTING HOUSE TO MULTINATIONAL COMPANIES.

BECOMING A COMMUNITY ORGANIZER, A DREAM FROM HIS COLLEGE DAYS, WAS SLIPPING FARTHER AWAY BY THE DAY.

THEN ONE DAY HE RECEIVED A PHONE CALL FROM SOMEONE NAMED AUMA.

AUMA WAS AN AFRICAN HALF-SISTER OBAMA HAD NEVER MET. SHE HAD LEFT KENYA TO STUDY IN GERMANY. NOW SHE WAS COMING TO THE U.S. WITH FRIENDS, AND WANTED TO VISIT BARACK IN NEW YORK.

OF COURSE. YOU CAN STAY WITH ME, I CAN'T WAIT.

HE SPENT WEEKS PREPARING FOR COMPANY.

TWO DAYS BEFORE HER ARRIVAL, THOUGH, HE GOT ANOTHER CALL.

I CAN'T COME AFTER ALL. ONE OF OUR BROTHERS, DAVID... HE'S BEEN KILLED. IN A MOTORCYCLE ACCIDENT.

OH, BARACK. WHY DO THESE THINGS HAPPEN TO US?

BARACK TOOK THE REST OF THE DAY OFF AND WALKED THE STREETS OF MANHATTAN, THINKING ABOUT FAMILY HE HAD NEVER KNOWN, ABOUT HIS LATE FATHER, WHO HAD DIED IN 1982, WHO HE HAD ONLY MET ONCE SINCE HIS SECOND YEAR.

THINKING ABOUT THE NECESSITY OF DOING WHAT HIS HEART TOLD HIM HE SHOULD, WHILE HE STILL HAD TIME.

WITHIN MONTHS, HE HAD RESIGNED HIS CORPORATE JOB AND BEGAN LOOKING FOR WORK AS A COMMUNITY ORGANIZER.

10

IN 1985 OBAMA MOVED TO CHICAGO.

HIRED BY THE DEVELOPING COMMUNITIES PROJECT, HE WENT TO WORK ON THE CITY'S IMPOVERISHED SOUTH SIDE. NOT ALL HIS EFFORTS PANNED OUT OR WERE MET WITH MUCH FANFARE.

BUT SOME DID—MORE AND MORE AS THE MONTHS PASSED HE BECAME BETTER KNOWN IN CHICAGO'S ACTIVIST COMMUNITY.

HE LEARNED TO LISTEN TO PEOPLE, TO DRAW OUT THEIR STORIES ABOUT THEMSELVES AND THEIR LIVES—AND IN TURN, TO TELL STORIES OF HIS OWN PERSONAL EXPERIENCES AS WELL AS HIS HOPES AND EXPECTATIONS FOR THE FUTURE.

THESE STORIES HELPED HIM FIND THE SENSE OF PURPOSE HE HAD BEEN SEEKING FOR SO LONG.

ORGANIZING IN THE COMMUNITY, OBAMA FOUND HIMSELF IN MANY CHURCHES, WORKING HAND-IN-HAND WITH THE CLERGY.

SEVERAL PASTORS TOLD HIM HE SHOULD MEET REVEREND JEREMIAH A. WRIGHT, JR. OF TRINITY UNITED CHURCH OF CHRIST.

FREE SOUTH AFRICA

SORRY FOR BEING LATE. WE'RE TRYING TO BUILD A NEW SANCTUARY, AND I HAD TO MEET WITH THE BANKERS.

I'M TELLING YOU, DOC, THEY ALWAYS WANT SOMETHING ELSE FROM YOU. LATEST THING IS ANOTHER LIFE INSURANCE POLICY ON ME. IN CASE I DROP DEAD TOMORROW. THEY FIGURE THE WHOLE CHURCH'LL COLLAPSE WITHOUT ME.

IS IT TRUE?

I'M NOT THE CHURCH, BARACK. IF I DIE TOMORROW, I HOPE THE CONGREGATION WILL GIVE ME A DECENT BURIAL. I LIKE TO THINK A FEW TEARS WILL BE SHED.

BUT AS SOON AS I'M SIX FEET UNDER, THEY'LL BE RIGHT BACK ON THE CASE, FIGURING OUT HOW TO MAKE THIS CHURCH LIVE UP TO ITS MISSION.

IMPRESSED WITH THE CHURCH'S SOCIAL ACTIVISM AND GROWING CONGREGATION, BARACK, WHO HAD NOT BEEN RAISED IN ANY ORGANIZED RELIGION, CONTINUED EXPLORING OTHER CHURCHES BUT FOUND HIMSELF DRAWN BACK TO TRINITY.

WRIGHT'S SERMON THAT SUNDAY, PARTLY INSPIRED BY ANOTHER PASTOR'S RECOLLECTION OF A PAINTING, WAS TITLED "THE AUDACITY OF HOPE."

THE PAINTING DEPICTS A HARPIST, A WOMAN WHO AT FIRST GLANCE APPEARS TO BE SITTING ATOP A GREAT MOUNTAIN.

UNTIL YOU TAKE A CLOSER LOOK AND SEE THAT THE WOMAN IS BRUISED AND BLOODIED, DRESSED IN TATTERED RAGS, THE HARP REDUCED TO A SINGLE FRAYED STRING.

YOUR EYE IS THEN DRAWN DOWN TO THE SCENE BELOW, DOWN TO THE VALLEY BELOW, WHERE EVERYWHERE ARE THE RAVAGES OF FAMINE, THE DRUMBEAT OF WAR, A WORLD GROANING UNDER STRIFE AND DEPRIVATION.

IT IS THIS WORLD, A WORLD WHERE CRUISE SHIPS THROW AWAY MORE FOOD IN A DAY THAN MOST RESIDENTS OF PORT-AU-PRINCE SEE IN A YEAR, WHERE WHITE FOLKS' GREED RUNS A WORLD IN NEED, APARTHEID IN ONE HEMISPHERE, APATHY IN ANOTHER HEMISPHERE... THAT'S THE WORLD! ON WHICH HOPE SITS!

AT LAST, BARACK OBAMA HAD FOUND A FAITH HE COULD EMBRACE.

BEFORE ENTERING HARVARD LAW SCHOOL, OBAMA VISITED HIS ANCESTRAL HOME IN KENYA.

HIS HALF-SISTER AUMA HAD FINALLY VISITED HIM IN CHICAGO AND THAT VISIT CONVINCED HIM HE NEEDED TO MAKE THE JOURNEY TO KENYA TO MEET THE REST OF HIS FAMILY.

TO SEE THE PLACE THAT HAD SHAPED HIS FATHER.

OBAMA'S STEP-GRANDMOTHER, WHO HE CALLED GRANNY, RELATED STORIES OF HIS GRANDFATHER'S LIFE, AND HIS FATHER'S—HEADSTRONG MEN MAKING THEIR WAY IN AN AFRICA UNDER WHITE COLONIAL RULE, FORCED INTO THE AFFAIRS OF THE 20TH CENTURY BY WAR AND COMMERCE, BUT TRYING TO CLING TO THEIR TRADITIONAL WAYS.

GRANNY STILL HAD THE REGISTER THAT OBAMA'S GRANDFATHER USED TO RECORD ALL HIS DOMESTIC SERVANT JOBS, AND LETTERS HIS FATHER HAD WRITTEN TO UNIVERSITIES ALL OVER THE UNITED STATES—THE LETTERS THAT EVENTUALLY GAINED HIM ADMITTANCE TO THE UNIVERSITY OF HAWAII.

DOMESTIC SERVANTS POCKET REGISTRY

OBAMA RECOGNIZED HIS LEGACY IN THE STORIES AND ARTIFACTS OF THESE MEN. THE THINGS THEY HAD PASSED DOWN.

HE LATER WROTE, "I REALIZED THAT WHO I WAS, WHAT I CARED ABOUT, WAS NO LONGER JUST A MATTER OF INTELLECT OR OBLIGATION, NO LONGER A CONSTRUCT OF WORDS.

"I SAW THAT MY LIFE IN AMERICA—THE BLACK LIFE, THE WHITE LIFE, THE SENSE OF ABANDONMENT I'D FELT AS A BOY, THE FRUSTRATION AND HOPE I'D WITNESSED IN CHICAGO—ALL OF IT WAS CONNECTED WITH THIS SMALL PLOT OF EARTH AN OCEAN AWAY, CONNECTED BY MORE THAN THE ACCIDENT OF A NAME OR THE COLOR OF MY SKIN.

"THE PAIN I FELT WAS MY FATHER'S PAIN. MY QUESTIONS WERE MY BROTHERS' QUESTIONS. THEIR STRUGGLE, MY BIRTHRIGHT."

BACK IN THE STATES, AFTER THE PIVOTAL KENYA TRIP, BARACK OBAMA ATTENDED HARVARD LAW SCHOOL.

ALTHOUGH HE OFTEN FOUND THE LAW DRY AND DISSATISFYING, REFLECTING DECISIONS THAT HAD MORE TO DO WITH GREED OR CONVENIENCE THAN COMPASSION OR TRUTH, HE EXCELLED AT IT.

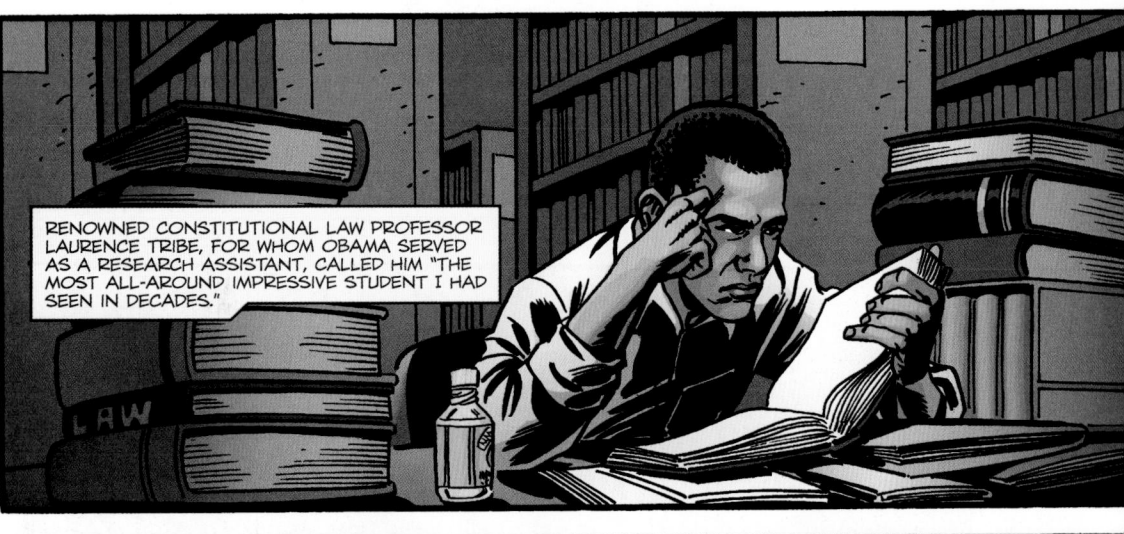

RENOWNED CONSTITUTIONAL LAW PROFESSOR LAURENCE TRIBE, FOR WHOM OBAMA SERVED AS A RESEARCH ASSISTANT, CALLED HIM "THE MOST ALL-AROUND IMPRESSIVE STUDENT I HAD SEEN IN DECADES."

IN 1990, BARACK BECAME THE FIRST AFRICAN-AMERICAN PRESIDENT OF THE HARVARD LAW REVIEW IN THAT PRESTIGIOUS INSTITUTION'S LONG HISTORY.

BEFORE GRADUATING MAGNA CUM LAUDE, HE HAD ALREADY RECEIVED A CONTRACT TO WRITE HIS MEMOIR, *DREAMS FROM MY FATHER*, AND BECOME ONE OF THE MOST PROMINENT LAW STUDENTS IN THE COUNTRY.

BUT CHICAGO BECKONED. WITH MORE THAN 600 OFFERS BEFORE GRADUATION, HE COULD HAVE WORKED FOR ALMOST ANY LAW FIRM IN THE NATION, BUT HE WANTED TO RETURN TO HIS ADOPTED CITY AND A CAREER IN PUBLIC-INTEREST LAW.

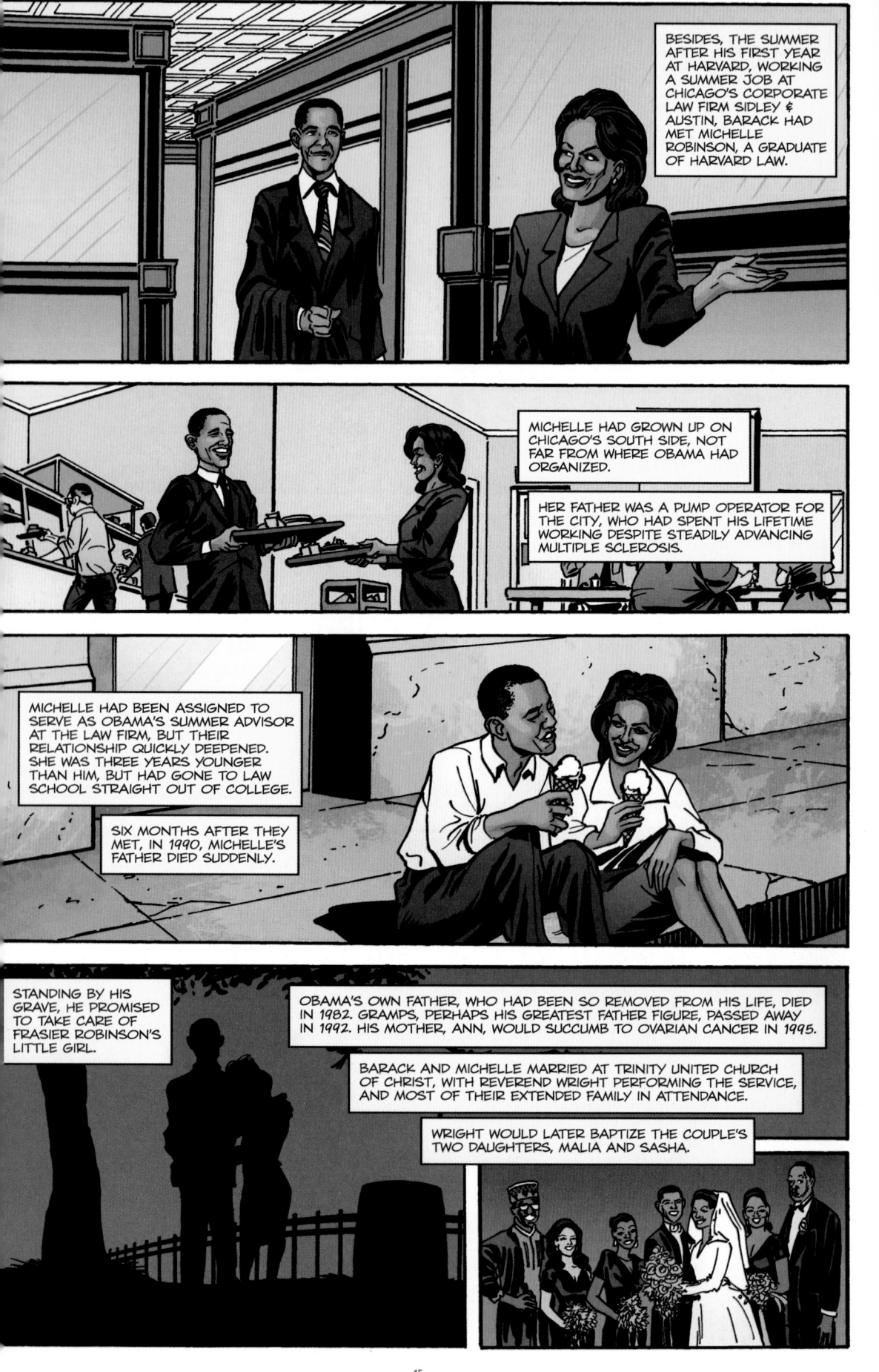

BESIDES, THE SUMMER AFTER HIS FIRST YEAR AT HARVARD, WORKING A SUMMER JOB AT CHICAGO'S CORPORATE LAW FIRM SIDLEY & AUSTIN, BARACK HAD MET MICHELLE ROBINSON, A GRADUATE OF HARVARD LAW.

MICHELLE HAD GROWN UP ON CHICAGO'S SOUTH SIDE, NOT FAR FROM WHERE OBAMA HAD ORGANIZED.

HER FATHER WAS A PUMP OPERATOR FOR THE CITY, WHO HAD SPENT HIS LIFETIME WORKING DESPITE STEADILY ADVANCING MULTIPLE SCLEROSIS.

MICHELLE HAD BEEN ASSIGNED TO SERVE AS OBAMA'S SUMMER ADVISOR AT THE LAW FIRM, BUT THEIR RELATIONSHIP QUICKLY DEEPENED. SHE WAS THREE YEARS YOUNGER THAN HIM, BUT HAD GONE TO LAW SCHOOL STRAIGHT OUT OF COLLEGE.

SIX MONTHS AFTER THEY MET, IN 1990, MICHELLE'S FATHER DIED SUDDENLY.

STANDING BY HIS GRAVE, HE PROMISED TO TAKE CARE OF FRASIER ROBINSON'S LITTLE GIRL.

OBAMA'S OWN FATHER, WHO HAD BEEN SO REMOVED FROM HIS LIFE, DIED IN 1982. GRAMPS, PERHAPS HIS GREATEST FATHER FIGURE, PASSED AWAY IN 1992. HIS MOTHER, ANN, WOULD SUCCUMB TO OVARIAN CANCER IN 1995.

BARACK AND MICHELLE MARRIED AT TRINITY UNITED CHURCH OF CHRIST, WITH REVEREND WRIGHT PERFORMING THE SERVICE, AND MOST OF THEIR EXTENDED FAMILY IN ATTENDANCE.

WRIGHT WOULD LATER BAPTIZE THE COUPLE'S TWO DAUGHTERS, MALIA AND SASHA.

IN CHICAGO, MARRIED AND PAYING OFF STUDENT LOANS, OBAMA WORKED AS AN ASSOCIATE ATTORNEY FOR THE LAW FIRM MINER BARNHILL & GALLAND, AND TAUGHT CONSTITUTIONAL LAW AT THE UNIVERSITY OF CHICAGO LAW SCHOOL.

MICHELLE WORKED AT CHICAGO'S DEPARTMENT OF PLANNING AND THEN RAN THE LOCAL BRANCH OF PUBLIC ALLIES, A NATIONAL SERVICE PROGRAM.

BY 1996, HOWEVER, HE HAD MADE THE DIFFICULT DECISION TO CAMPAIGN FOR POLITICAL OFFICE, RUNNING FOR A SEAT IN THE ILLINOIS SENATE. THE LEGISLATURE WAS DOMINATED BY REPUBLICANS AND HE RAN AS A DEMOCRAT FROM THE 13TH DISTRICT.

IN TRADITIONAL CHICAGO STYLE, THE CANDIDATE PLAYED HARDBALL POLITICS, USING TECHNICALITIES OF THE RULES TO KNOCK POTENTIAL OPPONENTS OUT OF THE RACE BY CHALLENGING THEIR BALLOT PETITIONS–EMPLOYING THE STRICTEST INTERPRETATION OF THE LAW TO BENEFIT HIS CAMPAIGN.

HE WON BY A LARGE MARGIN, AND WHEN HE WENT TO SPRINGFIELD IN JANUARY 1997, HE QUICKLY ESTABLISHED A REPUTATION AS A STATE SENATOR ABLE TO WORK ACROSS THE AISLE.

WORKING WITH SENATORS OF BOTH PARTIES, HE HELPED CRAFT AMBITIOUS CAMPAIGN FINANCE REFORM LEGISLATION THAT MADE HIS STATE ONE OF THE NATION'S BEST IN TERMS OF CAMPAIGN FINANCE DISCLOSURE.

OBAMA SPEARHEADED A BILL REQUIRING VIDEOTAPED HOMICIDE INTERROGATIONS AND CONFESSIONS, AND ANOTHER MONITORING RACIAL PROFILING IN TRAFFIC STOPS.

IN ADDITION TO WORKING HARD, HE PLAYED HARD, PLAYING POKER IN THE EVENINGS WITH LEGISLATORS OF EVERY PARTY AND POLITICAL CREED.

IN 2000, OBAMA SUFFERED HIS ONLY POLITICAL LOSS SO FAR, WHICH HE TERMED A "DRUBBING," WHEN HE RAN FOR A SEAT IN THE U.S. HOUSE OF REPRESENTATIVES AGAINST INCUMBENT BOBBY RUSH, A FORMER MEMBER OF THE BLACK PANTHERS.

WHEN THE RESULTS OF OBAMA'S INTERNAL POLLING CAME IN, RUSH'S NAME RECOGNITION WAS AT 90%. OBAMA'S WAS 11%. RUSH'S APPROVAL RATING WAS 70%, BUT OBAMA'S—AMONG PEOPLE WHO HAD HEARD OF HIM—WAS 8%.

IT WASN'T LONG BEFORE OBAMA KNEW HE WAS IN A LOSING BATTLE. BUT HE HAD TO KEEP FIGHTING TO THE END, AND IN SPITE OF A LATE SURGE, HE LOST BY 31 POINTS.

THE LOSS WAS NOT ONLY HUMILIATING, IT WAS EXPENSIVE, DEVASTATING HIS SAVINGS AND PERSONAL CREDIT.

IN HIS SECOND BOOK, *THE AUDACITY OF HOPE*, OBAMA RECOUNTED HIS TRIP TO LOS ANGELES FOR THE 2000 DEMOCRATIC NATIONAL CONVENTION...

I'M SORRY, MR. OBAMA, BUT YOUR CARD'S BEEN REJECTED.

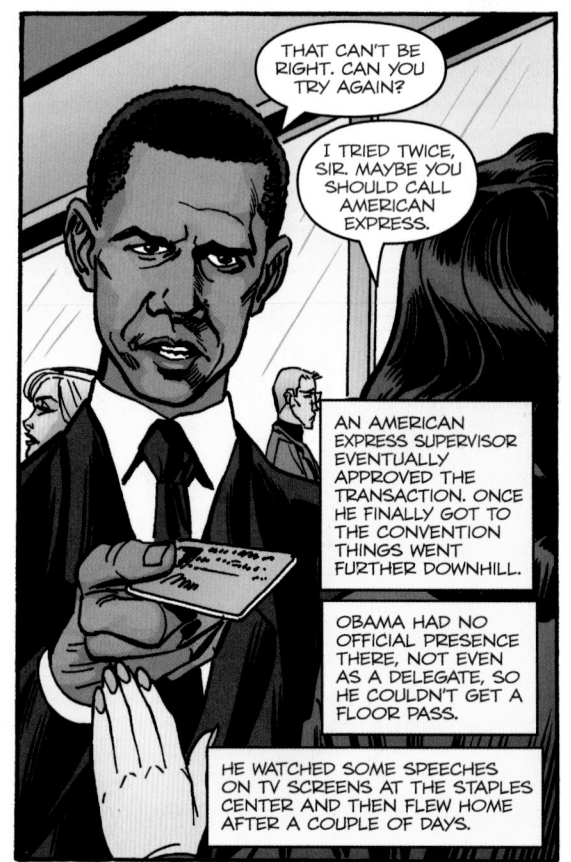

THAT CAN'T BE RIGHT. CAN YOU TRY AGAIN?

I TRIED TWICE, SIR. MAYBE YOU SHOULD CALL AMERICAN EXPRESS.

AN AMERICAN EXPRESS SUPERVISOR EVENTUALLY APPROVED THE TRANSACTION. ONCE HE FINALLY GOT TO THE CONVENTION THINGS WENT FURTHER DOWNHILL.

OBAMA HAD NO OFFICIAL PRESENCE THERE, NOT EVEN AS A DELEGATE, SO HE COULDN'T GET A FLOOR PASS.

HE WATCHED SOME SPEECHES ON TV SCREENS AT THE STAPLES CENTER AND THEN FLEW HOME AFTER A COUPLE OF DAYS.

AFTER WEIGHING HIS POLITICAL OPTIONS, OBAMA DECIDED TO STAY IN THE ILLINOIS SENATE, AND WON REELECTION IN 2002.

BUT EVEN THEN, HE WAS BEGINNING TO THINK ABOUT HIS NEXT STEP—THE U.S. SENATE. HE STARTED MAKING APPEARANCES AROUND THE STATE, TRYING TO IMPROVE HIS NAME RECOGNITION.

THEN ON OCTOBER 2, 2002, HE GAVE WHAT WOULD BECOME ONE OF THE MOST IMPORTANT SPEECHES OF HIS POLITICAL CAREER, BEFORE A GROUP OF PEOPLE OPPOSING THE COMING WAR IN IRAQ.

LET ME BEGIN BY SAYING THAT ALTHOUGH THIS HAS BEEN BILLED AS AN ANTI-WAR RALLY, I STAND BEFORE YOU AS SOMEONE WHO IS NOT OPPOSED TO WAR IN ALL CIRCUMSTANCES.

THE CIVIL WAR WAS ONE OF THE BLOODIEST IN HISTORY, AND YET IT WAS ONLY THROUGH THE CRUCIBLE OF THE SWORD, THE SACRIFICE OF MULTITUDES, THAT WE COULD BEGIN TO PERFECT THIS UNION, AND DRIVE THE SCOURGE OF SLAVERY FROM OUR SOIL.

I DON'T OPPOSE ALL WARS.

WHAT I AM OPPOSED TO IS A DUMB WAR. WHAT I AM OPPOSED TO IS A RASH WAR. WHAT I AM OPPOSED TO IS THE CYNICAL ATTEMPT BY RICHARD PERLE AND PAUL WOLFOWITZ AND OTHER ARMCHAIR,

NO WAR IN IRAQ

WEEKEND WARRIORS IN THIS ADMINISTRATION TO SHOVE THEIR OWN IDEOLOGICAL AGENDAS DOWN OUR THROATS, IRRESPECTIVE OF THE COSTS IN LIVES LOST AND IN HARDSHIPS BORNE.

WHAT I AM OPPOSED TO IS THE ATTEMPT BY POLITICAL HACKS LIKE KARL ROVE TO DISTRACT US FROM A RISE IN THE UNINSURED, A RISE IN THE POVERTY RATE, A DROP IN THE MEDIAN INCOME—TO DISTRACT US FROM CORPORATE SCANDALS AND A STOCK MARKET THAT HAS JUST GONE THROUGH THE WORST MONTH SINCE THE GREAT DEPRESSION.

THAT'S WHAT I'M OPPOSED TO. A DUMB WAR. A RASH WAR. A WAR BASED NOT ON REASON BUT ON PASSION, NOT ON PRINCIPLE BUT ON POLITICS.

I KNOW THAT EVEN A SUCCESSFUL WAR AGAINST IRAQ WILL REQUIRE A U.S. OCCUPATION OF UNDETERMINED LENGTH, AT UNDETERMINED COST, WITH UNDETERMINED CONSEQUENCES.

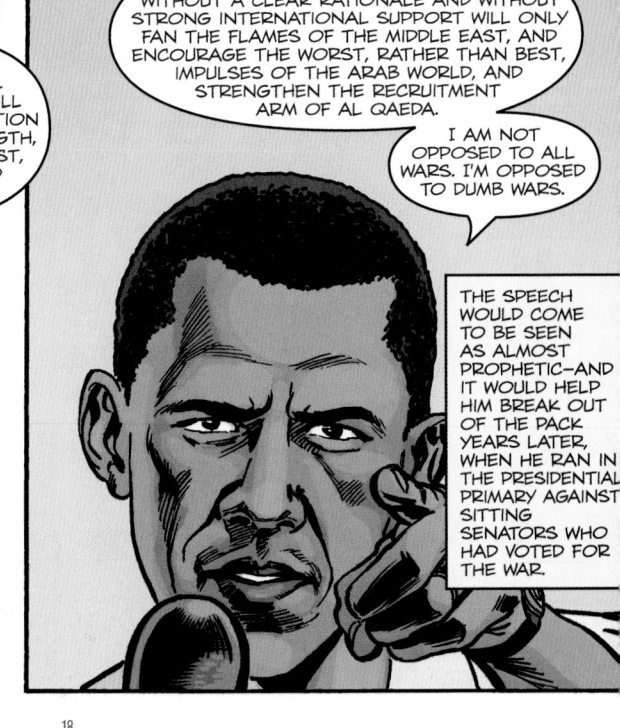

I KNOW THAT AN INVASION OF IRAQ WITHOUT A CLEAR RATIONALE AND WITHOUT STRONG INTERNATIONAL SUPPORT WILL ONLY FAN THE FLAMES OF THE MIDDLE EAST, AND ENCOURAGE THE WORST, RATHER THAN BEST, IMPULSES OF THE ARAB WORLD, AND STRENGTHEN THE RECRUITMENT ARM OF AL QAEDA.

I AM NOT OPPOSED TO ALL WARS. I'M OPPOSED TO DUMB WARS.

THE SPEECH WOULD COME TO BE SEEN AS ALMOST PROPHETIC—AND IT WOULD HELP HIM BREAK OUT OF THE PACK YEARS LATER, WHEN HE RAN IN THE PRESIDENTIAL PRIMARY AGAINST SITTING SENATORS WHO HAD VOTED FOR THE WAR.

MICHELLE WASN'T CONVINCED THAT POLITICS WAS A PROFESSION FOR HONORABLE PEOPLE. SHE AGREED TO A SENATE RUN, THOUGH, WHICH WOULD BE OBAMA'S LAST HURRAH IF HE DIDN'T WIN.

HE APPLIED THE LESSONS OF 2000. HE WORKED HARD, AND HE GOT LUCKY, CATCHING BREAKS THAT HAD FALLEN THE OTHER WAY IN HIS CONGRESSIONAL BID.

HIS BIGGEST BREAK WAS WHEN HIS ORIGINAL REPUBLICAN OPPONENT, JACK RYAN, WAS FORCED OUT BY PERSONAL SCANDAL AND THE STATE PARTY, DESPERATE, BROUGHT IN ALAN KEYES, WHO HAD NEVER LIVED IN ILLINOIS AND HAD NEVER WON AN ELECTION.

WE GOT OUR OWN HARVARD-EDUCATED CONSERVATIVE BLACK GUY TO GO UP AGAINST THE HARVARD-EDUCATED LIBERAL BLACK GUY. HE MAY NOT WIN, BUT AT LEAST HE CAN KNOCK THAT HALO OFF YOUR HEAD.

IN ANOTHER BREAK, HE WAS INVITED TO PROVIDE THE KEYNOTE ADDRESS FOR THE 2004 DEMOCRATIC NATIONAL CONVENTION NOMINATING JOHN KERRY.

GIVEN HIS ONLY PREVIOUS EXPERIENCE AT THE PARTY'S CONVENTION, IN 2000, HE APPROACHED IT WITH SOME ANXIETY.

THIS TIME, EVERYTHING HAD TO BE RIGHT.

AND EVERYTHING WAS RIGHT. WITHIN MINUTES AFTER THE 17-MINUTE SPEECH BEGAN, PEOPLE EVERYWHERE—IN THE BOSTON HALL AND WATCHING ON PRIME-TIME TV—WERE PAYING ATTENTION TO THE RELATIVELY UNKNOWN SENATORIAL CANDIDATE FROM ILLINOIS.

I STAND HERE KNOWING THAT MY STORY IS PART OF THE LARGER AMERICAN STORY, THAT I OWE A DEBT TO ALL OF THOSE WHO CAME BEFORE ME, AND THAT, IN NO OTHER COUNTRY ON EARTH, IS MY STORY EVEN POSSIBLE.

TONIGHT, WE GATHER TO AFFIRM THE GREATNESS OF OUR NATION NOT BECAUSE OF THE HEIGHT OF OUR SKYSCRAPERS, OR THE POWER OF OUR MILITARY, OR THE SIZE OF OUR ECONOMY.

OUR PRIDE IS BASED ON A VERY SIMPLE PREMISE, SUMMED UP IN A DECLARATION MADE OVER TWO HUNDRED YEARS AGO, "WE HOLD THESE TRUTHS TO BE SELF-EVIDENT, THAT ALL MEN ARE CREATED EQUAL.

"THAT THEY ARE ENDOWED BY THEIR CREATOR WITH CERTAIN INALIENABLE RIGHTS. THAT AMONG THESE ARE LIFE, LIBERTY AND THE PURSUIT OF HAPPINESS."

NOW EVEN AS WE SPEAK, THERE ARE THOSE WHO ARE PREPARING TO DIVIDE US, THE SPIN MASTERS AND NEGATIVE AD PEDDLERS WHO EMBRACE THE POLITICS OF ANYTHING GOES.

WELL, I SAY TO THEM TONIGHT, THERE'S NOT A LIBERAL AMERICA AND A CONSERVATIVE AMERICA— THERE'S THE UNITED STATES OF AMERICA. THERE'S NOT A BLACK AMERICA AND WHITE AMERICA AND LATINO AMERICA AND ASIAN AMERICA—THERE'S THE UNITED STATES OF AMERICA.

THE PUNDITS LIKE TO SLICE-AND-DICE OUR COUNTRY INTO RED STATES AND BLUE STATES; RED STATES FOR REPUBLICANS, BLUE STATES FOR DEMOCRATS. BUT I'VE GOT NEWS FOR THEM, TOO.

WE WORSHIP AN AWESOME GOD IN THE BLUE STATES, AND WE DON'T LIKE FEDERAL AGENTS POKING AROUND OUR LIBRARIES IN THE RED STATES. WE COACH LITTLE LEAGUE IN THE BLUE STATES AND, YES, WE'VE GOT SOME GAY FRIENDS IN THE RED STATES.

THERE ARE PATRIOTS WHO OPPOSED THE WAR IN IRAQ AND THERE ARE PATRIOTS WHO SUPPORTED THE WAR IN IRAQ. WE ARE ONE PEOPLE, ALL OF US PLEDGING ALLEGIANCE TO THE STARS AND STRIPES, ALL OF US DEFENDING THE UNITED STATES OF AMERICA.

BY THE NEXT DAY, BARACK OBAMA WAS A ROCK STAR.

THE NEW YORK TIMES WROTE:

"AS HE MOVED THROUGH ROOMS AND HALLWAYS, WHISPERS FOLLOWED: PERHAPS THE MAN WHO HAD JUST PASSED WOULD BE THE FIRST BLACK PRESIDENT OF THE UNITED STATES."

BACK IN ILLINOIS, THE CROWDS FOR HIS CAMPAIGN RALLIES BALLOONED.

JOHN KERRY LOST HIS PRESIDENTIAL BID, BUT IN A BRIGHT SPOT FOR DEMOCRATS THAT NOVEMBER, BARACK OBAMA WAS SWEPT INTO THE SENATE.

HE WAS THE FIFTH AFRICAN-AMERICAN SENATOR IN U.S. HISTORY, ONLY THE THIRD TO BE POPULARLY ELECTED.

HE QUICKLY FOUND HIMSELF RECOGNIZED EVERYWHERE—EVEN AT A WHITE HOUSE EVENT...

YOU'VE GOT A BRIGHT FUTURE. VERY BRIGHT. BUT I'VE BEEN IN THIS TOWN AWHILE AND, LET ME TELL YOU, IT CAN BE TOUGH. WHEN YOU GET A LOT OF ATTENTION LIKE YOU'VE BEEN GETTING, PEOPLE START GUNNIN' FOR YA.

AND IT WON'T NECESSARILY JUST BE COMING FROM MY SIDE, YOU UNDERSTAND. FROM YOURS, TOO. EVERYBODY'LL BE WAITING FOR YOU TO SLIP, KNOW WHAT I MEAN? SO WATCH YOURSELF.

THANKS FOR THE ADVICE, MR. PRESIDENT.

YOU KNOW, ME AND YOU GOT SOMETHING IN COMMON. WE BOTH HAD TO DEBATE ALAN KEYES. THAT GUY'S A PIECE OF WORK, ISN'T HE?

AS IN ILLINOIS, HE SET RIGHT TO WORK, MASTERING THE ISSUES AND CROSSING PARTY LINES ON SIGNIFICANT LEGISLATION—WORKING WITH REPUBLICANS RICHARD LUGAR ON NUCLEAR NONPROLIFERATION, TOM COBURN ON TRANSPARENCY IN GOVERNMENT CONTRACTING, AND JOHN McCAIN ON BORDER SECURITY, IMMIGRATION AND GREENHOUSE GAS REDUCTIONS.

DURING HIS SENATE CAREER HE HAS SERVED ON COMMITTEES FOR FOREIGN RELATIONS, VETERAN'S AFFAIRS, HEALTH, EDUCATION, LABOR AND PENSIONS, AND HOMELAND SECURITY AND GOVERNMENTAL AFFAIRS.

AFTER OBAMA'S SENATE VICTORY, HIS FIRST BOOK WAS REISSUED AND HIS SECOND ONE, *THE AUDACITY OF HOPE*, CONTRACTED. THEIR FINANCIAL FORTUNES SECURE, THE OBAMAS PAID OFF STUDENT LOANS AND BOUGHT A NEW $1.6 MILLION HOUSE IN CHICAGO'S POSH KENWOOD.

BUT OBAMA'S SELF-DESCRIBED "RESTLESSNESS" PULLED HIM TOWARD A NEW GOAL, SPURRED ON BY SUPPORTERS LIKE THE ILLINOIS SENIOR SENATOR RICHARD DURBIN...

...AND ON FEBRUARY 10, 2007, BEFORE THE OLD STATE CAPITOL IN SPRINGFIELD, IL, WHERE ABRAHAM LINCOLN MADE HIS HISTORIC "HOUSE DIVIDED" SPEECH, BARACK OBAMA ANNOUNCED HIS CAMPAIGN FOR THE PRESIDENCY OF THE UNITED STATES.

IT WAS HERE, IN SPRINGFIELD, WHERE NORTH, SOUTH, EAST AND WEST COME TOGETHER THAT I WAS REMINDED OF THE ESSENTIAL DECENCY OF THE AMERICAN PEOPLE—WHERE I CAME TO BELIEVE THAT THROUGH THIS DECENCY, WE CAN BUILD A MORE HOPEFUL AMERICA.

AND THAT IS WHY, IN THE SHADOW OF THE OLD STATE CAPITOL, WHERE LINCOLN ONCE CALLED ON A DIVIDED HOUSE TO STAND TOGETHER, WHERE COMMON HOPES AND COMMON DREAMS STILL LIVE, I STAND BEFORE YOU TODAY TO ANNOUNCE MY CANDIDACY FOR PRESIDENT OF THE UNITED STATES.

THE DEMOCRATIC FIELD WAS CROWDED, WITH FORMER FIRST LADY SENATOR HILLARY CLINTON, THE ACKNOWLEDGED FRONTRUNNER.

ALSO RUNNING WERE SENATORS JOE BIDEN, CHRIS DODD, FORMER SENATORS JOHN EDWARDS AND MIKE GRAVEL, GOVERNORS BILL RICHARDSON AND TOM VILSACK, AND CONGRESSMAN DENNIS KUCINICH.

BY THE FIRST OFFICIAL DEMOCRATIC DEBATE IN SOUTH CAROLINA, ON APRIL 26, 2007, VILSACK HAD DROPPED OUT, BUT THE REST SHARED THE STAGE.

OBAMA'S FIRST WORDS REMINDED THE AUDIENCE OF HIS EARLY OPPOSITION TO WAR IN IRAQ.

WELL, BRIAN, I AM PROUD THAT I OPPOSED THIS WAR FROM THE START, BECAUSE I THOUGHT THAT IT WOULD LEAD TO THE DISASTROUS CONDITIONS THAT WE'VE SEEN ON THE GROUND IN IRAQ.

AS CAMPAIGN MANAGER, OBAMA CHOSE LONG-TIME ALLY DAVID PLOUFFE, WITH DAVID AXELROD AS MEDIA CONSULTANT AND ROBERT GIBBS AS COMMUNICATIONS DIRECTOR.

FROM THE BEGINNING, THE CANDIDATE DECLARED THIS WOULD BE A DIFFERENT SORT OF RACE, WITH NO NEGATIVE CAMPAIGNING—ALTHOUGH AS THE RACE TIGHTENED THAT DECLARATION WOULD EVENTUALLY LOOSEN.

ADDITIONALLY, OBAMA ACCEPTED NO CONTRIBUTIONS FROM PAID LOBBYISTS OR POLITICAL ACTION COMMITTEES. IN SPITE OF THIS, HE SET NEW FUNDRAISING RECORDS, RAISING MILLIONS ONLINE AND FROM SMALL DONORS.

THROUGH THE LONG SUMMER AND FALL OF 2007, HE PRESSED HARD, BUT SO DID THE OTHER FRONTRUNNERS, CLINTON AND EDWARDS. CLINTON CONTINUED TO LEAD IN THE POLLS. OBAMA WAS HOUNDED BY CHARGES THAT HE WASN'T EXPERIENCED ENOUGH.

HE COUNTERED BY SAYING THAT EXPERIENCE AT THE NATIONAL LEVEL WAS NO SUBSTITUTE FOR GOOD JUDGMENT, OR THE KIND OF LIFE EXPERIENCE HE'D HAD AS AN ACTIVIST, ORGANIZER, AND STATE SENATOR.

HIS BIOGRAPHY WAS HIS BIGGEST ASSET.

I THINK THAT IF YOU CAN TELL PEOPLE, "WE HAVE A PRESIDENT IN THE WHITE HOUSE WHO STILL HAS A GRANDMOTHER LIVING IN A HUT ON THE SHORES OF LAKE VICTORIA AND HAS A SISTER WHO'S HALF-INDONESIAN, MARRIED TO A CHINESE-CANADIAN," THEN THEY'RE GOING TO THINK HE MAY HAVE A BETTER SENSE OF WHAT'S GOING ON IN OUR LIVES AND IN OUR COUNTRY. AND THEY'D BE RIGHT.

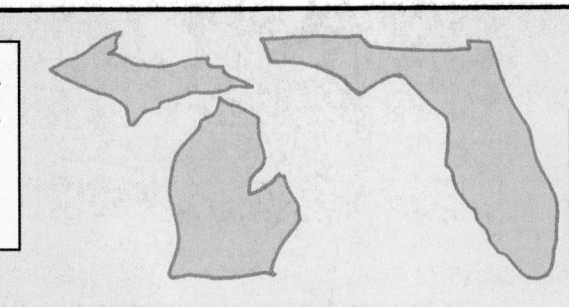

ONE OF THE CAMPAIGN'S BIGGEST CONTROVERSIES AROSE WHEN TWO STATES VIOLATED THE DEMOCRATIC NATIONAL COMMITTEE'S RULING THAT ONLY IOWA, NEW HAMPSHIRE, NEVADA, AND SOUTH CAROLINA COULD HOLD CONTESTS BEFORE FEBRUARY 5TH.

FLORIDA AND MICHIGAN DID SO, AND THE DEMOCRATIC CANDIDATES AGREED NOT TO CAMPAIGN IN THOSE STATES. OBAMA, BIDEN, EDWARDS, AND RICHARDSON REMOVED THEIR NAMES FROM THE MICHIGAN BALLOT.

OBAMA SCORED A DRAMATIC VICTORY IN THE IOWA CAUCUSES, WHERE RECORD-BREAKING TURNOUT HELPED HIM CARRY THE DAY.

HOPE—HOPE IS WHAT LED ME HERE TODAY. WITH A FATHER FROM KENYA, A MOTHER FROM KANSAS, AND A STORY THAT COULD ONLY HAPPEN IN THE UNITED STATES OF AMERICA.

HOPE IS THE BEDROCK OF THIS NATION. THE BELIEF THAT OUR DESTINY WILL NOT BE WRITTEN FOR US, BUT BY US, BY ALL THOSE MEN AND WOMEN WHO ARE NOT CONTENT TO SETTLE FOR THE WORLD AS IT IS, WHO HAVE THE COURAGE TO REMAKE THE WORLD AS IT SHOULD BE.

THE BIG WIN MADE HIM THE NEW FRONTRUNNER IN NEW HAMPSHIRE, BUT CLINTON CAME OUT NARROWLY AHEAD. BECAUSE OF PROPORTIONAL ALLOCATION OF DELEGATES, THE STATE WAS A VIRTUAL TIE.

CLINTON WON AGAIN IN NEVADA, BUT DELEGATE ALLOCATION RULES AWARDED MORE DELEGATES TO OBAMA. HE FOLLOWED THAT WITH A 2-TO-1 VICTORY IN SOUTH CAROLINA.

FLORIDA AND MICHIGAN CAME NEXT. HILLARY CLINTON CLAIMED VICTORY IN EACH, DESPITE THE UNRESOLVED CONTROVERSY BECAUSE BOTH STATES HAD JUMPED THE OFFICIAL PRIMARY SCHEDULE.

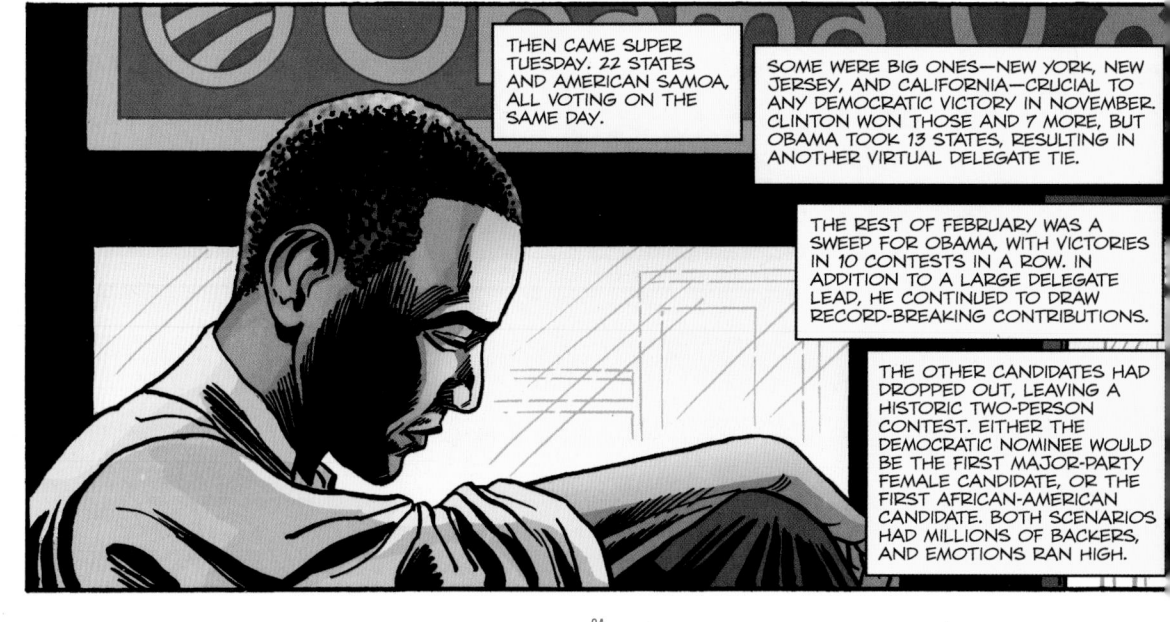

THEN CAME SUPER TUESDAY. 22 STATES AND AMERICAN SAMOA, ALL VOTING ON THE SAME DAY.

SOME WERE BIG ONES—NEW YORK, NEW JERSEY, AND CALIFORNIA—CRUCIAL TO ANY DEMOCRATIC VICTORY IN NOVEMBER. CLINTON WON THOSE AND 7 MORE, BUT OBAMA TOOK 13 STATES, RESULTING IN ANOTHER VIRTUAL DELEGATE TIE.

THE REST OF FEBRUARY WAS A SWEEP FOR OBAMA, WITH VICTORIES IN 10 CONTESTS IN A ROW. IN ADDITION TO A LARGE DELEGATE LEAD, HE CONTINUED TO DRAW RECORD-BREAKING CONTRIBUTIONS.

THE OTHER CANDIDATES HAD DROPPED OUT, LEAVING A HISTORIC TWO-PERSON CONTEST. EITHER THE DEMOCRATIC NOMINEE WOULD BE THE FIRST MAJOR-PARTY FEMALE CANDIDATE, OR THE FIRST AFRICAN-AMERICAN CANDIDATE. BOTH SCENARIOS HAD MILLIONS OF BACKERS, AND EMOTIONS RAN HIGH.

CONTROVERSY REARED UP AT DIFFERENT POINTS ALONG THE WAY—SOME SIGNIFICANT, OTHERS MANUFACTURED FOR POLITICAL EFFECT.

OBAMA DIDN'T ALWAYS WEAR A FLAG PIN ON HIS LAPEL, GENERATING CRITICISM FROM SOME QUARTERS.

FORMER PRESIDENT BILL CLINTON MADE A STATEMENT IN SOUTH CAROLINA THAT SOME CONSIDERED A RACIST ATTACK ON BARACK OBAMA.

GIVE ME A BREAK. THIS WHOLE THING IS THE BIGGEST FAIRY TALE I'VE EVER SEEN.

AND MICHELLE OBAMA RAN INTO TROUBLE FOR A COMMENT SHE MADE.

FOR THE FIRST TIME IN MY ADULT LIFETIME, I AM REALLY PROUD OF MY COUNTRY. AND NOT JUST BECAUSE BARACK HAS DONE WELL, BUT BECAUSE I THINK PEOPLE ARE HUNGRY FOR CHANGE. AND I HAVE BEEN DESPERATE TO SEE OUR COUNTRY MOVING IN THAT DIRECTION.

PAST RELATIONSHIPS CREATED PROBLEMS FOR OBAMA, TOO, INCLUDING ASSOCIATIONS WITH REAL ESTATE DEVELOPER TONY REZKO, ON TRIAL FOR FRAUD AND MONEY LAUNDERING. OBAMA HAS CHARACTERIZED A LAND DEAL BETWEEN THE TWO "A MISTAKE."

ALSO, FORMER WEATHER UNDERGROUND MEMBER AND ADMITTED BOMBER, WILLIAM AYERS HAS BEEN TERMED "OBAMA'S WILLIE HORTON."

THEN THERE WAS REV. WRIGHT...

THE GOVERNMENT GIVES THEM THE DRUGS, BUILDS BIGGER PRISONS, PASSES A THREE-STRIKE LAW AND THEN WANTS US TO SING 'GOD BLESS AMERICA.' NO, NO, NO, GOD DAMN AMERICA, THAT'S IN THE BIBLE FOR KILLING INNOCENT PEOPLE.

GOD DAMN AMERICA FOR TREATING OUR CITIZENS AS LESS THAN HUMAN. GOD DAMN AMERICA FOR AS LONG AS SHE ACTS LIKE SHE IS GOD AND SHE IS SUPREME.

ALTHOUGH ASSERTING HE WASN'T PRESENT FOR WRIGHT'S MOST INFLAMMATORY SERMONS, OBAMA RESPONDED TO THE REVELATIONS ABOUT THEM WITH A SPEECH ON RACE THAT WAS WIDELY CONSIDERED TO BE MAKE-OR-BREAK FOR HIS CAMPAIGN.

I CAN NO MORE DISOWN HIM THAN I CAN DISOWN THE BLACK COMMUNITY. I CAN NO MORE DISOWN HIM THAN I CAN MY WHITE GRANDMOTHER—A WOMAN WHO HELPED RAISE ME, A WOMAN WHO SACRIFICED AGAIN AND AGAIN FOR ME,

A WOMAN WHO LOVES ME AS MUCH AS SHE LOVES ANYTHING IN THIS WORLD, BUT A WOMAN WHO ONCE CONFESSED HER FEAR OF BLACK MEN WHO PASSED BY HER ON THE STREET, AND WHO ON MORE THAN ONE OCCASION HAS UTTERED RACIAL OR ETHNIC STEREOTYPES THAT MADE ME CRINGE.

LATER, HE WENT FURTHER, BREAKING ALL TIES WITH THE CHURCH.

ON APRIL 6TH, OBAMA CAUSED A STIR BY TALKING ABOUT RURAL VOTERS IN A WAY THAT WAS CHARACTERIZED AS ELITIST.

YOU GO INTO SOME OF THESE SMALL TOWNS IN PENNSYLVANIA, AND LIKE A LOT OF SMALL TOWNS IN THE MIDWEST, THE JOBS HAVE BEEN GONE NOW FOR 25 YEARS AND NOTHING'S REPLACED THEM.

AND THEY FELL THROUGH THE CLINTON ADMINISTRATION, AND THE BUSH ADMINISTRATION, AND EACH SUCCESSIVE ADMINISTRATION HAS SAID THAT SOMEHOW THESE COMMUNITIES ARE GONNA REGENERATE AND THEY HAVE NOT.

AND IT'S NOT SURPRISING, THEN, THAT THEY GET BITTER, THEY CLING TO GUNS OR RELIGION OR ANTIPATHY TOWARD PEOPLE WHO AREN'T LIKE THEM OR ANTI-IMMIGRANT SENTIMENT OR ANTI-TRADE SENTIMENT AS A WAY TO EXPLAIN THEIR FRUSTRATIONS.

IN SPITE OF THESE SETBACKS, THE PRIMARY SEASON CONTINUED TO BE A VIRTUAL DEAD HEAT, WITH BOTH OBAMA AND HILLARY CLINTON MARKING WINS.

SOME CALLED FOR CLINTON TO DROP OUT, AS OBAMA'S LEAD GREW. BUT SHE CONTINUED WINNING CONTESTS AND STAYED IN.

IN PORTLAND, OREGON, HE DREW THE LARGEST CROWD OF THE CAMPAIGN, WHEN 75,000 PEOPLE SHOWED UP FOR A RALLY.

THE BIG WIN IN OREGON, AND DELEGATES GATHERED IN HIS LOSS IN KENTUCKY, GAVE OBAMA A VIRTUALLY INSURMOUNTABLE LEAD IN PLEDGED DELEGATES.

ON MAY 31, THE DEMOCRATIC NATIONAL COMMITTEE'S RULES COMMITTEE MET TO END THE DEBATE OVER MICHIGAN AND FLORIDA.

THEY DECIDED TO SEAT THOSE DELEGATIONS AT HALF STRENGTH, DASHING CLINTON'S HOPES AND FIRMING UP OBAMA'S LEAD.

THE FINAL TWO PRIMARIES, IN SOUTH DAKOTA AND MONTANA, WERE HELD ON JUNE 3.

DURING THE DAY, A SLIDE OF SUPER-DELEGATES TOWARD OBAMA GUARANTEED HIM THE MAGIC NUMBER OF 2,118 DELEGATES NEEDED FOR THE NOMINATION, AND THE TV NETWORKS ANNOUNCED HIS WIN THE MINUTE POLLS CLOSED IN MONTANA. MSNBC ANCHOR KEITH OLBERMANN REFLECTED ON THE HISTORIC EVENT.

WE HAVE HURTLED ANOTHER BARRIER THAT SO MANY COUNTRIES HAVE FAILED TO DO, AND WE HAVE FAILED TO DO SO MANY TIMES. IT IS AN EXTRAORDINARY MOMENT.

ALTHOUGH DURING A CONFERENCE CALL THAT DAY CLINTON SAID SHE WOULD BE "OPEN" TO SERVING AS OBAMA'S RUNNING MATE, WHEN CLINTON SPOKE THAT EVENING, SHE DID NOT CONCEDE THE RACE.

I WILL BE MAKING NO DECISIONS TONIGHT.

OBAMA DIDN'T NEED SENATOR CLINTON TO CONCEDE BEFORE HE CLAIMED VICTORY, THOUGH. THE MATH WAS ON HIS SIDE.

BEFORE A CAPACITY CROWD AT THE XCEL CENTER IN ST. PAUL, MINNESOTA HE TOOK THE STAGE IN A JUBILANT MOOD.

TONIGHT, AFTER FIFTY-FOUR HARD-FOUGHT CONTESTS, OUR PRIMARY SEASON HAS FINALLY COME TO AN END. SIXTEEN MONTHS HAVE PASSED SINCE WE FIRST STOOD TOGETHER ON THE STEPS OF THE OLD STATE CAPITOL IN SPRINGFIELD, ILLINOIS.

THOUSANDS OF MILES HAVE BEEN TRAVELED. MILLIONS OF VOICES HAVE BEEN HEARD. AND BECAUSE OF WHAT YOU SAID—BECAUSE YOU DECIDED THAT CHANGE MUST COME TO WASHINGTON; BECAUSE YOU BELIEVED THAT THIS YEAR MUST BE DIFFERENT THAN ALL THE REST;

BECAUSE YOU CHOSE TO LISTEN NOT TO YOUR DOUBTS OR YOUR FEARS BUT TO YOUR GREATEST HOPES AND HIGHEST ASPIRATIONS, TONIGHT WE MARK THE END OF ONE HISTORIC JOURNEY WITH THE BEGINNING OF ANOTHER—A JOURNEY THAT WILL BRING A NEW AND BETTER DAY TO AMERICA.

TONIGHT, I CAN STAND BEFORE YOU AND SAY THAT I WILL BE THE DEMOCRATIC NOMINEE FOR PRESIDENT OF THE UNITED STATES.

CHANGE
WE CAN BELIEVE IN

WHETHER HE WINS THE PRESIDENCY OR NOT, BY BECOMING THE FIRST AFRICAN-AMERICAN CANDIDATE OF A MAJOR PARTY, WITH A GOOD SHOT AT THE WHITE HOUSE, BARACK OBAMA HAS ALREADY MADE HISTORY.

HE HAS FOUND THE PLACE HE BELONGS, THE COMMUNITY HE HAS SOUGHT FOR A LIFETIME, AND IT IS IN THE HEARTS AND MINDS OF MILLIONS OF AMERICAN VOTERS.

THE END

Written by Jeff Mariotte

Art by Tom Morgan

Color by Len O'Grady

Letters by Robbie Robbins

Cover art by J. Scott Campbell

Cover color by Edgar Delgado

Edited by Scott Dunbier

The cover pencils by artist J. Scott Campbell